WHAT'S INSIDE

AIRPLANES?

STEVE PARKER

PETER BEDRICK BOOKS

NEW YORK

Published by
PETER BEDRICK BOOKS
2112 Broadway
New York, NY 10023

Published by agreement with
Macdonald Young Books Ltd., England

Library of Congress Cataloging-in-
Publication Data

Parker, Steve.
What's inside airplanes? / Steve Parker.—1st
American ed.   p.   cm.—(What's inside series)
Includes index.
ISBN 0-87226-394-0
1. Airplanes—Juvenile literature. [1. Airplanes.
2. Aeronautics.] I. Title. II. Series: What's inside.
TL547.P273 1995
629.133'34—dc20
94-48544
CIP
AC

Commissioning Editor: Thomas Keegan
Designer: John Kelly
Editor: Nicky Barber
Illustrators: Kevin Maddison, Mark Franklin
and Frank Richards
Typesetters:
Goodfellow & Egan, Cambridge

First American edition 1995
Printed and bound in Hong Kong

Words in bold in the text can be found in
the Glossary on p.**44**

Contents

Introduction

On a clear day, near a big city or an airfield, you may see many different types of flying machines. Huge jetliners come and go. Military planes practice maneuvers. People take up their **light planes**, microlights, gliders and balloons. Helicopters hover over traffic jams.

How do these machines fly? What are the parts inside, and how do they work? This book looks inside airplanes and other flying machines, and helps you to find out the answers to these questions.

Lift

Faster-moving air creates lower pressure

Flat lower surface

Curved upper surface

THE AIRFOIL
The key to flight is the **airfoil** – the shape of the airplane wing. The upper surface is curved, the lower surface flatter. As the wing moves, air flowing over the top has farther to go, and it moves faster than the air flowing underneath. So the air pressure above the wing is less than below it, producing an upward force, or '**lift**'.

THE LIGHT PLANE
This typical small airplane is of the type known as a light plane. It has the same main parts as bigger planes.

Over the years, designers and engineers have found that the best layout for a plane is a central tube-shaped fuselage, two large wings near the middle, and two small wings plus an upright fin at the back.

Wing tip

Leading edge of wing

Cockpit or cabin

Windscreen

Propeller

Engine

Nose cone

Nose

Aileron
Flap
Trailing edge of wing

Pilot's seat
Passenger seat

Door   Wing root

Fuel tank
Landing gear

Fuselage

Rib of wing   Spar of wing

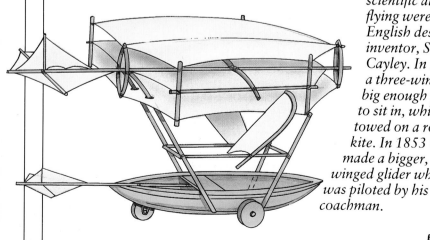

Cayley's glider

EARLY FLIERS
Some of the earliest scientific attempts at flying were made by an English designer and inventor, Sir George Cayley. In 1849 he built a three-winged glider big enough for a boy to sit in, which was towed on a rope like a kite. In 1853 Cayley made a bigger, single-winged glider which was piloted by his coachman.

HOVERCRAFT
Hovercraft 'fly', but only just. They glide on a cushion of air, and they can move over smooth land or across water. They make excellent passenger vehicles, needing only a beach or ramp on which to land.

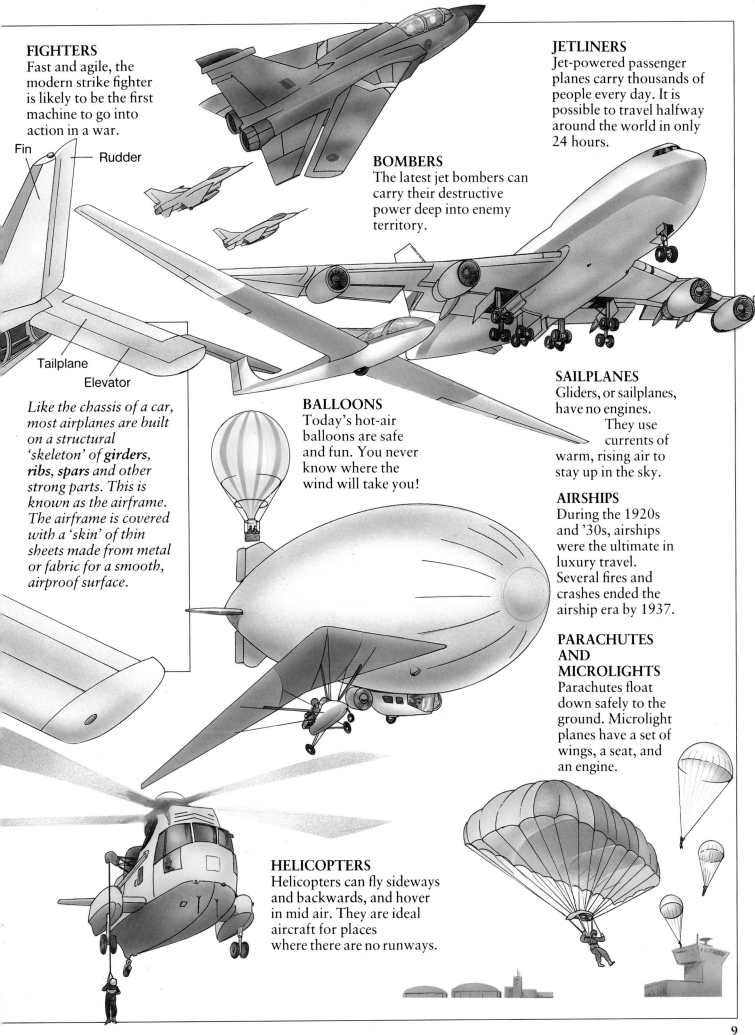

FIGHTERS
Fast and agile, the modern strike fighter is likely to be the first machine to go into action in a war.

Fin
Rudder

Tailplane
Elevator

*Like the chassis of a car, most airplanes are built on a structural 'skeleton' of **girders**, **ribs**, **spars** and other strong parts. This is known as the airframe. The airframe is covered with a 'skin' of thin sheets made from metal or fabric for a smooth, airproof surface.*

JETLINERS
Jet-powered passenger planes carry thousands of people every day. It is possible to travel halfway around the world in only 24 hours.

BOMBERS
The latest jet bombers can carry their destructive power deep into enemy territory.

SAILPLANES
Gliders, or sailplanes, have no engines. They use currents of warm, rising air to stay up in the sky.

AIRSHIPS
During the 1920s and '30s, airships were the ultimate in luxury travel. Several fires and crashes ended the airship era by 1937.

PARACHUTES AND MICROLIGHTS
Parachutes float down safely to the ground. Microlight planes have a set of wings, a seat, and an engine.

BALLOONS
Today's hot-air balloons are safe and fun. You never know where the wind will take you!

HELICOPTERS
Helicopters can fly sideways and backwards, and hover in mid air. They are ideal aircraft for places where there are no runways.

Pioneers in the sky

The 'age of the airplane' began on December 17, 1903, on a beach at Kitty Hawk, North Carolina, USA. The *Flyer I*, designed and built by brothers Orville and Wilbur Wright, was the first true airplane. It became the first heavier-than-air craft to achieve controlled, sustained flight. Some newspapers of the time thought that the Wright brothers' flight was a joke. Little did they realize how airplanes would change the world.

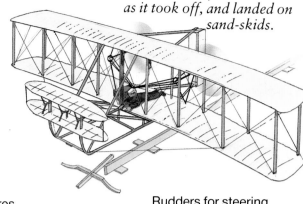

The Flyer *gained speed on a small buggy that ran on iron rails. It left this behind as it took off, and landed on sand-skids.*

Bracing wires

Rudders for steering

Rudder supports

THE *FLYER*
The *Flyer*'s first flight was piloted by Orville Wright. It lasted 12 seconds, covering 118 feet at a height of about 10 feet. Later on the same day another flight lasted 59 seconds.

Elevator

Engine

Controls

Chain link from engine to propeller

Muslin fabric covering

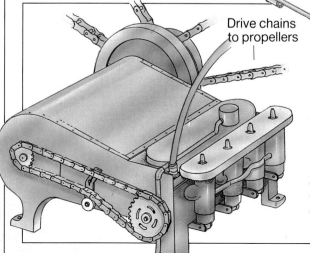

Drive chains to propellers

THE *FLYER*'S ENGINE
The steam and gasoline engines being built at the beginning of the 20th century were too heavy for planes. The Wrights, who were bicycle engineers, designed and built their own lightweight, four-cylinder gasoline engine. It produced about 15 horsepower (an average family car engine produces about 80 horsepower).

The Wrights chose the Kitty Hawk test area because of its strong, steady and reliable winds, which helped to give the Flyer *extra lift.*

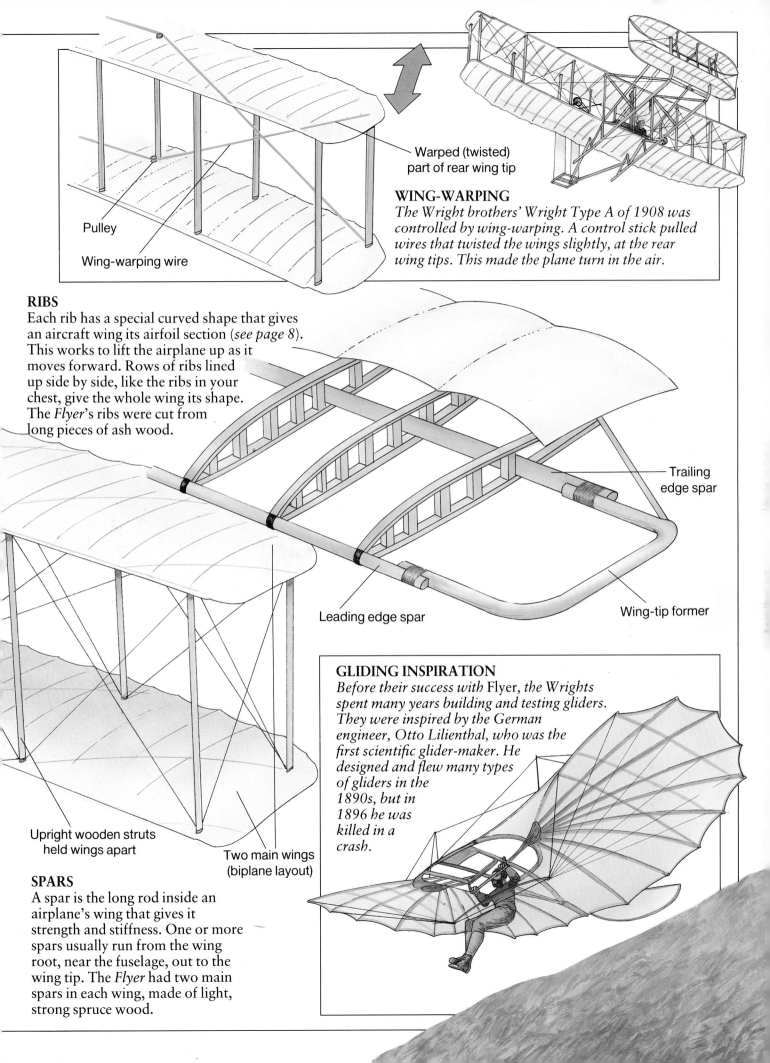

Pulley

Wing-warping wire

Warped (twisted)
part of rear wing tip

WING-WARPING
*The Wright brothers' Wright Type A of 1908 was
controlled by wing-warping. A control stick pulled
wires that twisted the wings slightly, at the rear
wing tips. This made the plane turn in the air.*

RIBS
Each rib has a special curved shape that gives
an aircraft wing its airfoil section (*see page 8*).
This works to lift the airplane up as it
moves forward. Rows of ribs lined
up side by side, like the ribs in your
chest, give the whole wing its shape.
The *Flyer*'s ribs were cut from
long pieces of ash wood.

Trailing
edge spar

Leading edge spar

Wing-tip former

GLIDING INSPIRATION
Before their success with Flyer, *the Wrights
spent many years building and testing gliders.
They were inspired by the German
engineer, Otto Lilienthal, who was the
first scientific glider-maker. He
designed and flew many types
of gliders in the
1890s, but in
1896 he was
killed in a
crash.*

Upright wooden struts
held wings apart

Two main wings
(biplane layout)

SPARS
A spar is the long rod inside an
airplane's wing that gives it
strength and stiffness. One or more
spars usually run from the wing
root, near the fuselage, out to the
wing tip. The *Flyer* had two main
spars in each wing, made of light,
strong spruce wood.

The first air travelers

Air travel really took off in the 1920s. Cars were becoming more common too, but they were relatively slow, and many roads were rough and full of holes. The early passenger planes offered astonishingly fast journeys, at 100 miles per hour! Compared to today's planes, however, they were noisy and slow. Flights were often cancelled because of fog, high winds or heavy rain. Yet rich people lined up to fly in these early airliners.

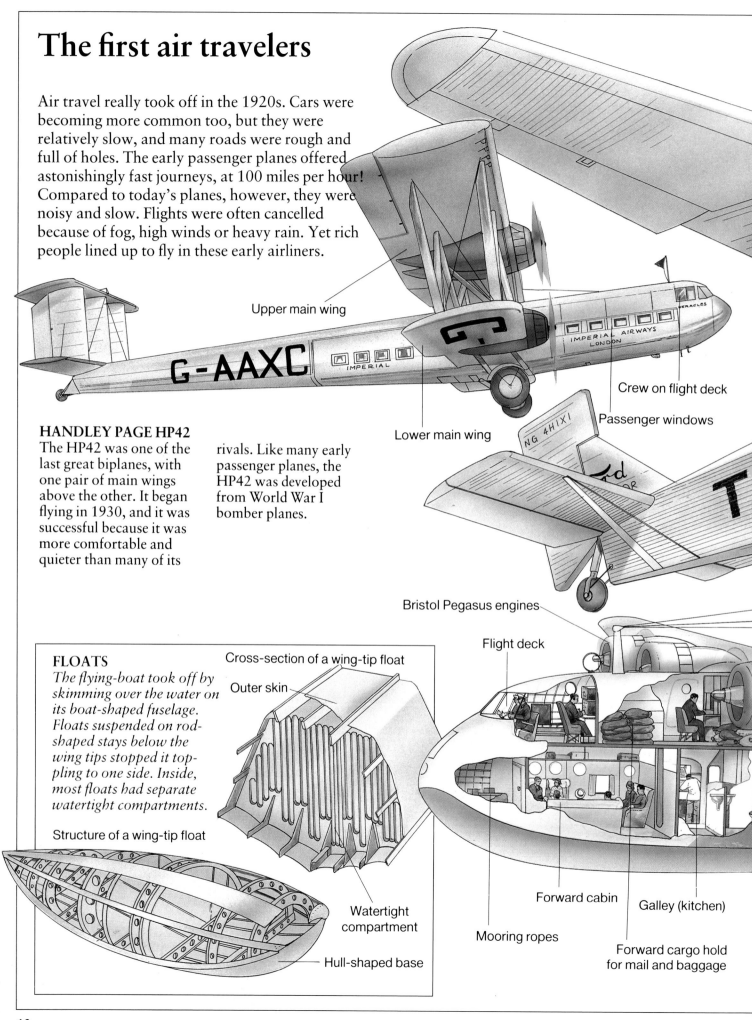

Upper main wing

G-AAXC

IMPERIAL

IMPERIAL AIRWAYS
LONDON

Lower main wing

Crew on flight deck

Passenger windows

HANDLEY PAGE HP42
The HP42 was one of the last great biplanes, with one pair of main wings above the other. It began flying in 1930, and it was successful because it was more comfortable and quieter than many of its rivals. Like many early passenger planes, the HP42 was developed from World War I bomber planes.

Bristol Pegasus engines

Flight deck

FLOATS
The flying-boat took off by skimming over the water on its boat-shaped fuselage. Floats suspended on rod-shaped stays below the wing tips stopped it toppling to one side. Inside, most floats had separate watertight compartments.

Cross-section of a wing-tip float

Outer skin

Structure of a wing-tip float

Watertight compartment

Hull-shaped base

Forward cabin

Galley (kitchen)

Mooring ropes

Forward cargo hold for mail and baggage

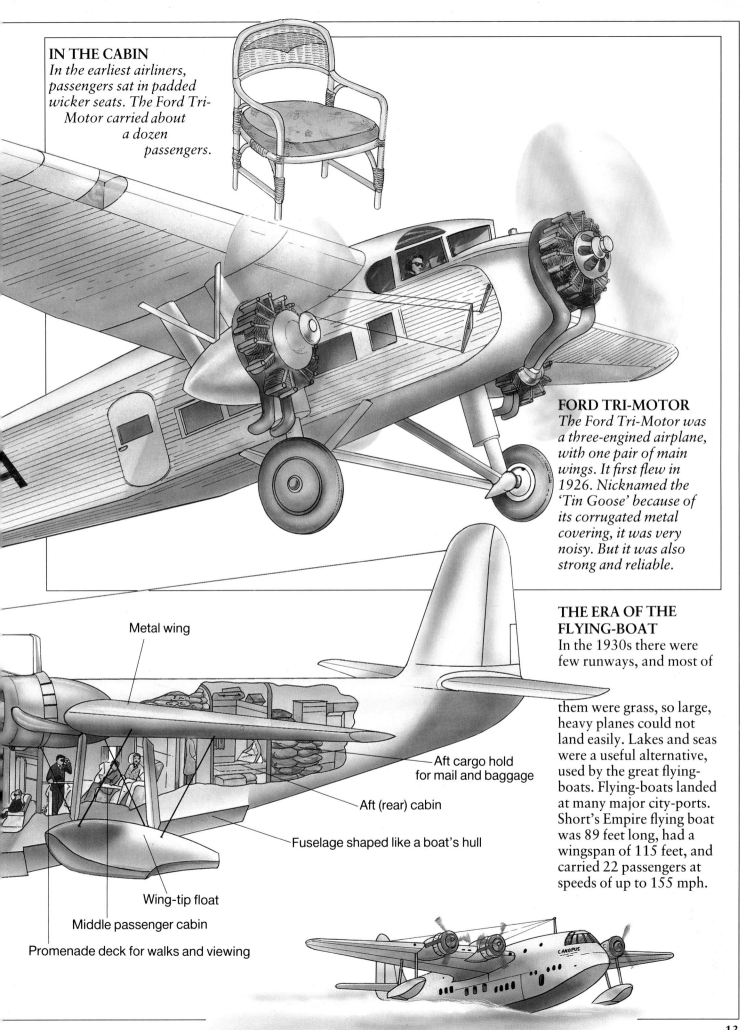

IN THE CABIN
In the earliest airliners, passengers sat in padded wicker seats. The Ford Tri-Motor carried about a dozen passengers.

FORD TRI-MOTOR
The Ford Tri-Motor was a three-engined airplane, with one pair of main wings. It first flew in 1926. Nicknamed the 'Tin Goose' because of its corrugated metal covering, it was very noisy. But it was also strong and reliable.

Metal wing

Aft cargo hold for mail and baggage

Aft (rear) cabin

Fuselage shaped like a boat's hull

Wing-tip float

Middle passenger cabin

Promenade deck for walks and viewing

THE ERA OF THE FLYING-BOAT
In the 1930s there were few runways, and most of them were grass, so large, heavy planes could not land easily. Lakes and seas were a useful alternative, used by the great flying-boats. Flying-boats landed at many major city-ports. Short's Empire flying boat was 89 feet long, had a wingspan of 115 feet, and carried 22 passengers at speeds of up to 155 mph.

Pistons and propellers

Ever since the Wright brothers' first flight in 1903, there have been airplanes powered by **piston** engines turning **propellers**. Jet planes became common from the 1940s. But 'prop planes' are still used around the world. The piston engines in airplanes have many similarities with those in cars, motorcycles, boats, small generators and many other machines.

INSIDE THE ENGINE

The typical plane engine has a number of cylindrical pistons – four are shown here – that move up and down in chambers called **cylinders**. They are connected to a main crankshaft and spin it around. This turns the propeller.

The piston (*above right*) has a series of rings around it, that make a good seal with the walls of the cylinder. This prevents exploding gases from the fuel-and-air mixture in the cylinder leaking out.

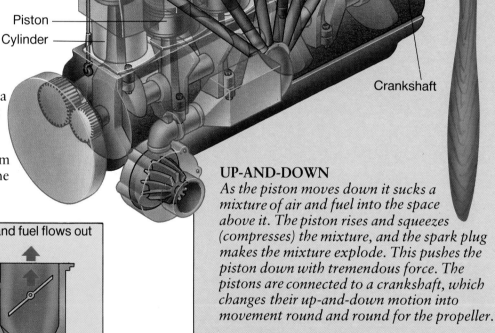

Compression piston rings

Oil-control piston ring

Oil-scraper piston ring

Piston head

Propeller

Piston pin

Piston tail

Engine casing

Piston

Cylinder

Crankshaft

UP-AND-DOWN

As the piston moves down it sucks a mixture of air and fuel into the space above it. The piston rises and squeezes (compresses) the mixture, and the spark plug makes the mixture explode. This pushes the piston down with tremendous force. The pistons are connected to a crankshaft, which changes their up-and-down motion into movement round and round for the propeller.

Piston 1 moves up

Fuel-air mixture compressed

Piston 2 forced down

Fuel-air mixture explodes

Rotary motion of crankshaft

Mixture of air and fuel flows out

Spray nozzle

Float

Fuel pipe

Air flows in

Needle valve lets in fuel

FUEL CONTROL

The carburetor mixes gasoline with air and feeds the mixture to the engine. The fuel is sprayed through a tiny nozzle into the air going into the cylinders.

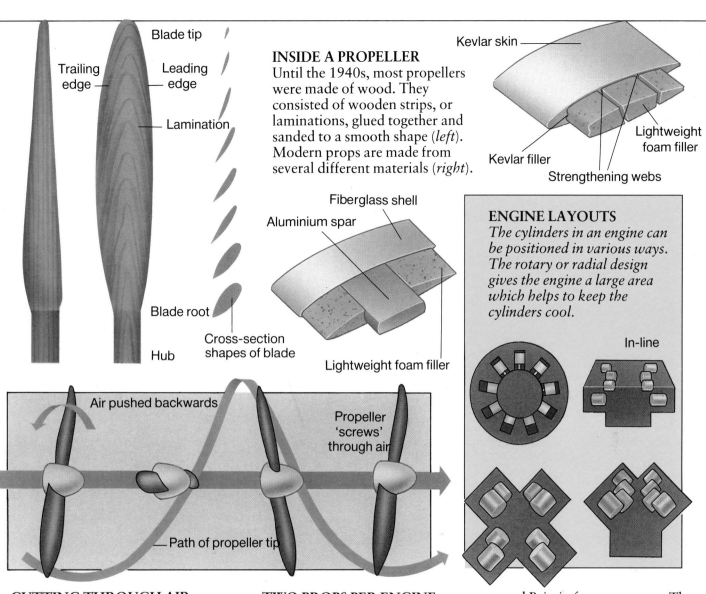

Trailing edge

Blade tip

Leading edge

Lamination

Blade root

Hub

Cross-section shapes of blade

INSIDE A PROPELLER

Until the 1940s, most propellers were made of wood. They consisted of wooden strips, or laminations, glued together and sanded to a smooth shape (*left*). Modern props are made from several different materials (*right*).

Kevlar skin

Kevlar filler

Strengthening webs

Lightweight foam filler

Fiberglass shell

Aluminium spar

Lightweight foam filler

ENGINE LAYOUTS

The cylinders in an engine can be positioned in various ways. The rotary or radial design gives the engine a large area which helps to keep the cylinders cool.

In-line

Air pushed backwards

Propeller 'screws' through air

Path of propeller tip

CUTTING THROUGH AIR

You may have felt cool air blown by the spinning blades of a fan, or seen the turning blades of a ship's propeller. An airplane propeller works in a similar way. Its angled blades cut through the air and push it backwards, so pulling the plane forwards.

TWO PROPS PER ENGINE

A few airplanes have two propellers on each engine, for example the Avro Shackleton, based on a World War II bomber. It flew 'sentry duty' on sea patrols around Britain for many years. The two props on each engine were contra-rotating. This means that they had blades angled to spin in opposite directions.

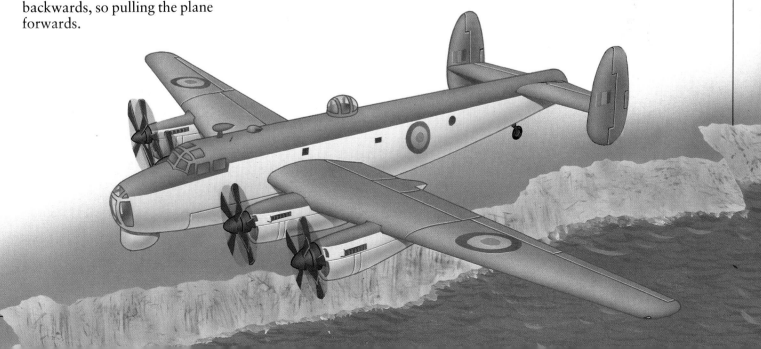

The 'arms' of the plane

The wings are the 'arms' of an airplane. They hold the plane aloft by creating lift from the air rushing over them (*see page 8*). Like all plane parts, the wings must be light and strong. Yet they should also be flexible, so that they can bend to absorb sudden gusts of wind, instead of cracking or snapping. The useful space inside the wing is taken up by control wires and cables, fuel tanks, landing gear, anti-icing and other equipment.

SPAR POSITIONS
The spars run along the length of the wing. They are positioned exactly where the bending forces and twisting stresses are greatest. There are usually more spars near the fuselage, where the wing's front-to-back distance, called the **chord**, is greatest.

WING DESIGN
The wing of a typical jetliner is swept back and gets narrower and thinner towards its tip. This gives good streamlining and lift at high speeds. The metal skin is only two millimeters (.08 inches) thick in places.

Wing tip

Outboard ribs

Holes for pipes, cables and wires

Trailing spar

Mid wings
Often used on aerobatic or stunt planes.

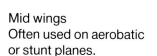

High wings
Good for stability but make position and folding of landing wheels awkward.

Low wings
Standard design for most modern airplanes, accepting fold-away landing wheels.

WING LAYOUTS
Early planes had relatively weak engines, so they needed to create maximum lift at low speeds. This came from two or even three sets of wings. There are several possible wing layouts depending on the plane's size, speed, construction and job.

Biplane

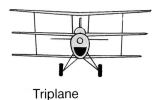

Triplane

HOLES IN RIBS
Many wires, cables and pipes pass along the wing, for example, the tubes leading from the fuel tanks, and the electrical wires for the wing-tip lights. These all pass through holes in the ribs. The holes are designed on a computer so that they reduce the weight of the rib without affecting its strength.

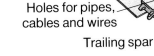

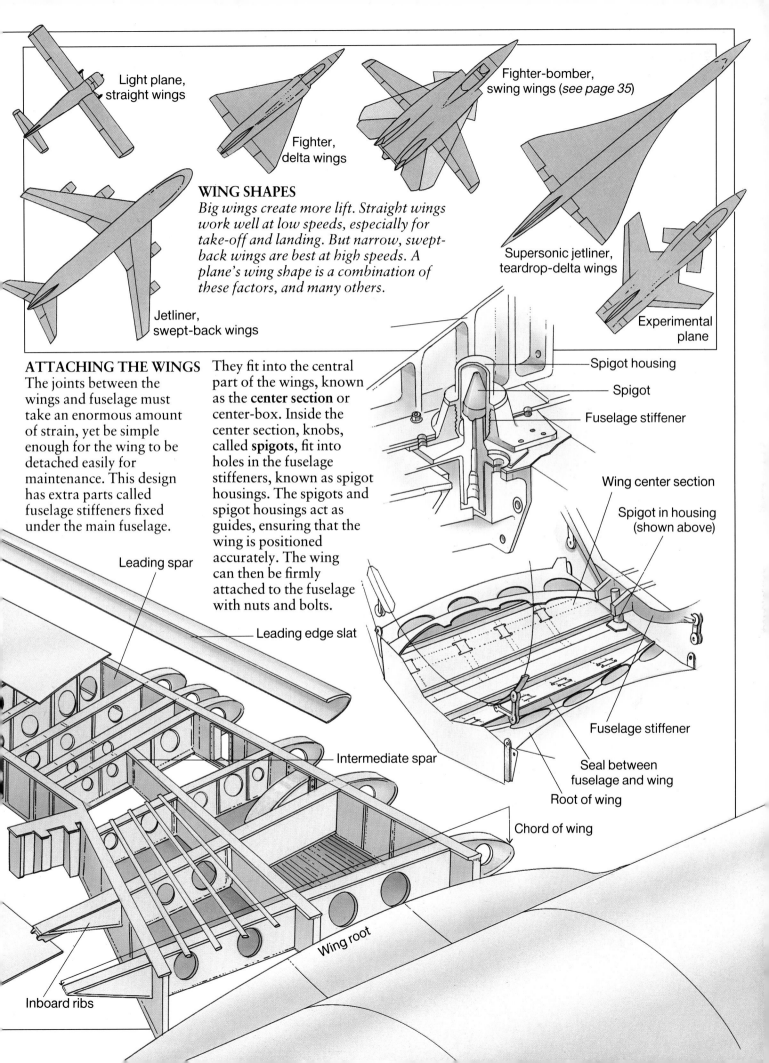

Light plane,
straight wings

Fighter,
delta wings

Fighter-bomber,
swing wings (*see page 35*)

WING SHAPES
Big wings create more lift. Straight wings work well at low speeds, especially for take-off and landing. But narrow, swept-back wings are best at high speeds. A plane's wing shape is a combination of these factors, and many others.

Supersonic jetliner,
teardrop-delta wings

Experimental
plane

Jetliner,
swept-back wings

ATTACHING THE WINGS
The joints between the wings and fuselage must take an enormous amount of strain, yet be simple enough for the wing to be detached easily for maintenance. This design has extra parts called fuselage stiffeners fixed under the main fuselage.

They fit into the central part of the wings, known as the **center section** or center-box. Inside the center section, knobs, called **spigots**, fit into holes in the fuselage stiffeners, known as spigot housings. The spigots and spigot housings act as guides, ensuring that the wing is positioned accurately. The wing can then be firmly attached to the fuselage with nuts and bolts.

Spigot housing

Spigot

Fuselage stiffener

Wing center section

Spigot in housing
(shown above)

Leading spar

Leading edge slat

Fuselage stiffener

Seal between
fuselage and wing

Root of wing

Intermediate spar

Chord of wing

Inboard ribs

Wing root

Turning and banking

As you come into land in a modern jetliner, try to look out of the window at the wing. You may be surprised at the number of panels and pieces that tilt and hinge away from the wing. These moving parts are called **control surfaces**. They change the flow of air over the wing in order to control the airplane's direction and its position in the air. They also alter the amount of lift produced at different speeds. The main control surfaces are the **flaps**, **ailerons**, **slats** and **spoilers**.

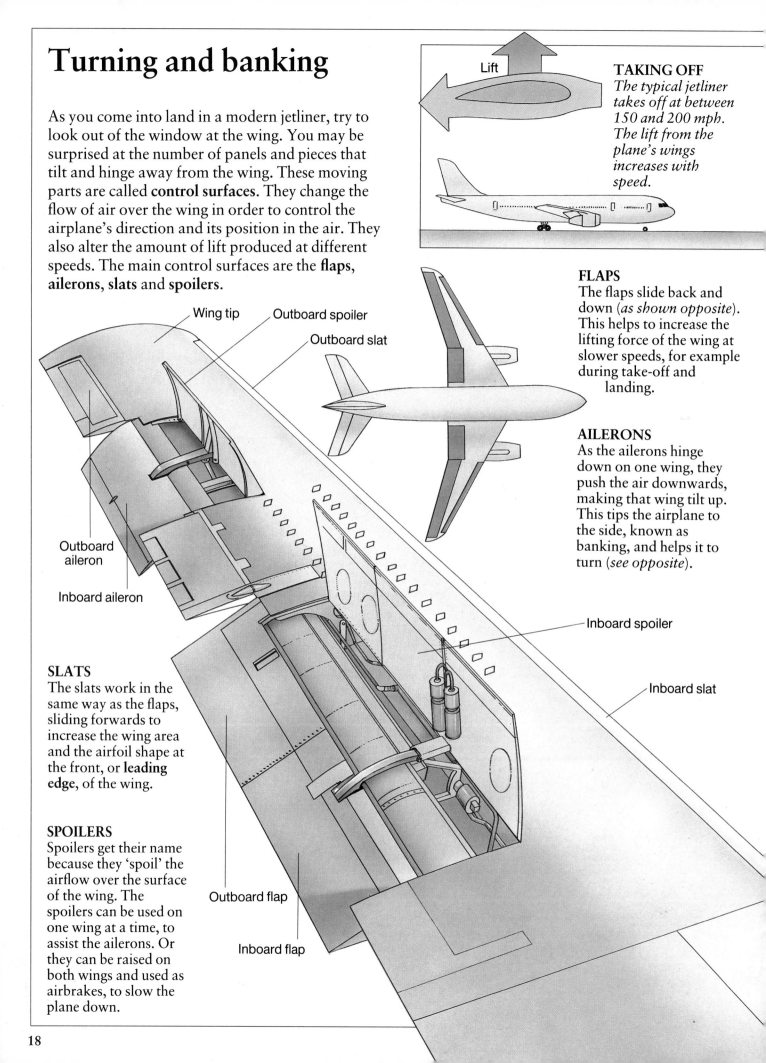

Wing tip

Outboard spoiler

Outboard slat

Outboard aileron

Inboard aileron

TAKING OFF
The typical jetliner takes off at between 150 and 200 mph. The lift from the plane's wings increases with speed.

Lift

FLAPS
The flaps slide back and down (*as shown opposite*). This helps to increase the lifting force of the wing at slower speeds, for example during take-off and landing.

AILERONS
As the ailerons hinge down on one wing, they push the air downwards, making that wing tilt up. This tips the airplane to the side, known as banking, and helps it to turn (*see opposite*).

Inboard spoiler

Inboard slat

SLATS
The slats work in the same way as the flaps, sliding forwards to increase the wing area and the airfoil shape at the front, or **leading edge**, of the wing.

SPOILERS
Spoilers get their name because they 'spoil' the airflow over the surface of the wing. The spoilers can be used on one wing at a time, to assist the ailerons. Or they can be raised on both wings and used as airbrakes, to slow the plane down.

Outboard flap

Inboard flap

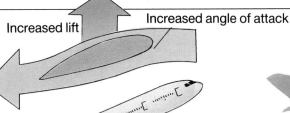

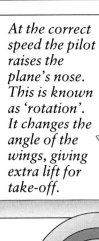

At the correct speed the pilot raises the plane's nose. This is known as 'rotation'. It changes the angle of the wings, giving extra lift for take-off.

Increased lift

Increased angle of attack

Angle of attack too great

If the nose comes up too much, the airflow over the wings breaks up. The plane stalls – tips up and then drops.

Lift greatly reduced

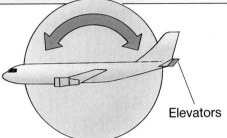

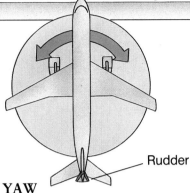

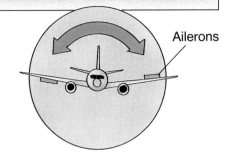

Elevators

Rudder

Ailerons

PITCH
An airplane can move in three directions. The first is called **pitch**, which means climbing up or diving down. Pitch is controlled mainly by the **elevators**.

YAW
Yaw means turning left or right, as when steering a car. It is controlled mainly by the **rudder** on the tail fin, as well as the ailerons (*see right*).

ROLL
Like a bicycle, a plane tilts, or banks, as it turns. This is called **roll**. This rolling is controlled by the ailerons.

FLAPS AND LIFT
Flaps slide out from the back of the wing, increasing its surface area. They also tilt down, increasing the curve of the wing. Both of these effects help to produce more lift at slower speeds.

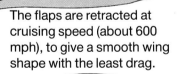

The flaps are retracted at cruising speed (about 600 mph), to give a smooth wing shape with the least drag.

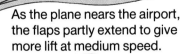

As the plane nears the airport, the flaps partly extend to give more lift at medium speed.

When the plan approaches the runway, the flaps fully extend to give most lift with less speed, so the landing is slower and safer.

OPERATING THE CONTROLS
The pilot operates the control surfaces by moving a control column or 'joystick' and foot pedals. The movements are transmitted by cables running around pulleys. However, in a big jetliner, the pilot's movements are fed through a series of gears, shafts and cables to **hydraulic jacks**. These move the control surfaces.

Air rushing past surface helps to push it back again

Jack forces surface out into airflow

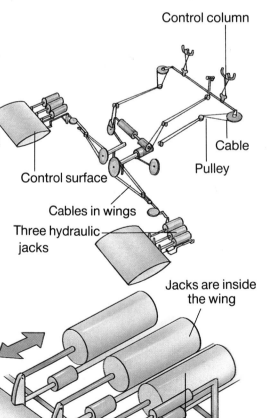

Control column

Cable

Pulley

Control surface

Cables in wings

Three hydraulic jacks

Jacks are inside the wing

Hydraulic jacks are pistons inside cylinders that contain fluid under high pressure.

Fuel and fuel tanks

As a huge jetliner thunders down the runway, taking off on a long-distance flight, it carries more than 100 tons of fuel. This is enough to drive a family car around the world over 30 times! But the fuel is not ordinary gasoline. It is special aviation-grade jet fuel, more like paraffin or kerosene. If there was a leak or crash, the fuel could easily catch alight. So the plane's fuel system includes many safety devices.

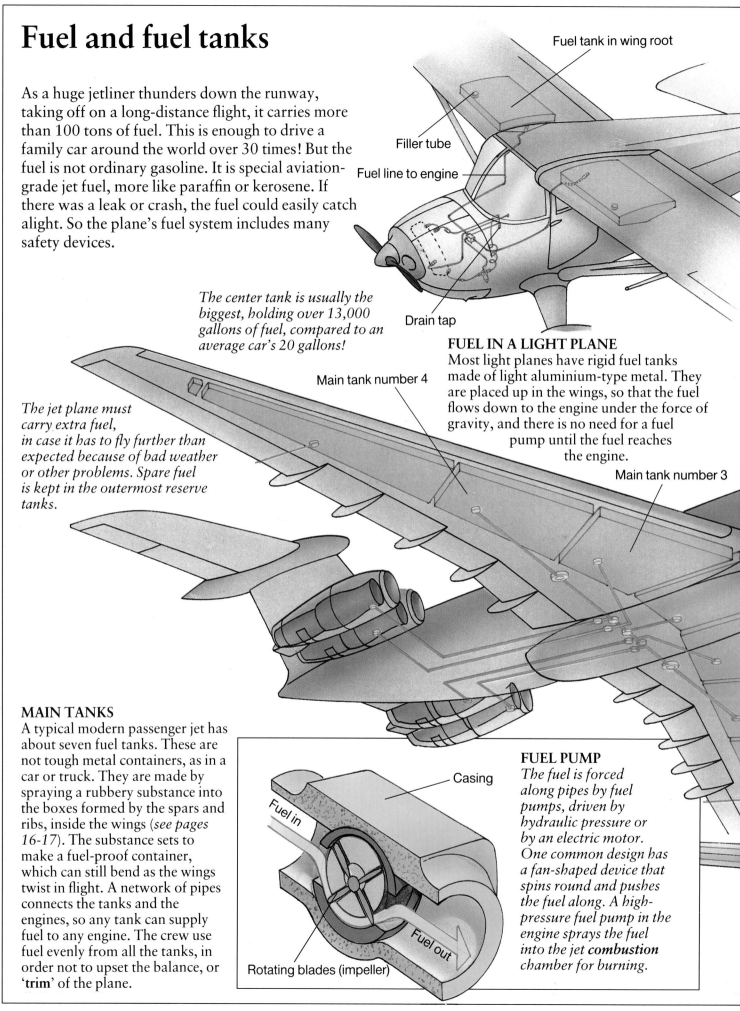

Fuel tank in wing root

Filler tube

Fuel line to engine

Drain tap

The center tank is usually the biggest, holding over 13,000 gallons of fuel, compared to an average car's 20 gallons!

Main tank number 4

The jet plane must carry extra fuel, in case it has to fly further than expected because of bad weather or other problems. Spare fuel is kept in the outermost reserve tanks.

FUEL IN A LIGHT PLANE
Most light planes have rigid fuel tanks made of light aluminium-type metal. They are placed up in the wings, so that the fuel flows down to the engine under the force of gravity, and there is no need for a fuel pump until the fuel reaches the engine.

Main tank number 3

MAIN TANKS
A typical modern passenger jet has about seven fuel tanks. These are not tough metal containers, as in a car or truck. They are made by spraying a rubbery substance into the boxes formed by the spars and ribs, inside the wings (*see pages 16-17*). The substance sets to make a fuel-proof container, which can still bend as the wings twist in flight. A network of pipes connects the tanks and the engines, so any tank can supply fuel to any engine. The crew use fuel evenly from all the tanks, in order not to upset the balance, or '**trim**' of the plane.

Casing

Fuel in

Fuel out

Rotating blades (impeller)

FUEL PUMP
*The fuel is forced along pipes by fuel pumps, driven by hydraulic pressure or by an electric motor. One common design has a fan-shaped device that spins round and pushes the fuel along. A high-pressure fuel pump in the engine sprays the fuel into the jet **combustion** chamber for burning.*

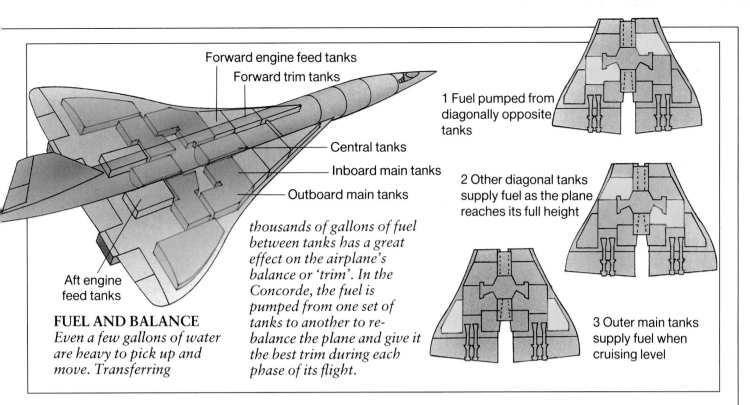

Forward engine feed tanks

Forward trim tanks

Central tanks

Inboard main tanks

Outboard main tanks

Aft engine
feed tanks

1 Fuel pumped from
diagonally opposite
tanks

2 Other diagonal tanks
supply fuel as the plane
reaches its full height

3 Outer main tanks
supply fuel when
cruising level

FUEL AND BALANCE
*Even a few gallons of water
are heavy to pick up and
move. Transferring*
*thousands of gallons of fuel
between tanks has a great
effect on the airplane's
balance or 'trim'. In the
Concorde, the fuel is
pumped from one set of
tanks to another to re-
balance the plane and give it
the best trim during each
phase of its flight.*

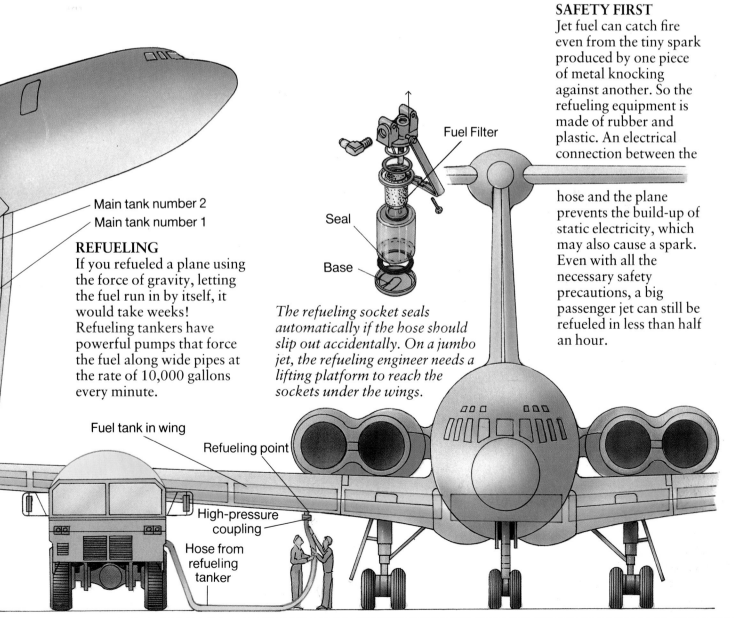

Main tank number 2

Main tank number 1

REFUELING
If you refueled a plane using
the force of gravity, letting
the fuel run in by itself, it
would take weeks!
Refueling tankers have
powerful pumps that force
the fuel along wide pipes at
the rate of 10,000 gallons
every minute.

Fuel Filter

Seal

Base

*The refueling socket seals
automatically if the hose should
slip out accidentally. On a jumbo
jet, the refueling engineer needs a
lifting platform to reach the
sockets under the wings.*

SAFETY FIRST
Jet fuel can catch fire
even from the tiny spark
produced by one piece
of metal knocking
against another. So the
refueling equipment is
made of rubber and
plastic. An electrical
connection between the
hose and the plane
prevents the build-up of
static electricity, which
may also cause a spark.
Even with all the
necessary safety
precautions, a big
passenger jet can still be
refueled in less than half
an hour.

Fuel tank in wing

Refueling point

High-pressure
coupling

Hose from
refueling
tanker

The power of the jet

There are several types of jet engines. Most modern big jetliners use **turbofan** jets, with a huge fan at the front. Turbofans are the quietest jet engines. This is especially useful for take-off and landing at airports near towns or cities. Turbofans also use the least fuel at normal cruising speeds of 500-600 mph. The first passenger jet to have turbofans was the Boeing 747 Jumbo, which came into service in 1969. At full power one of the latest turbofans produces as much power as 50 average family cars.

The engine is mounted under the wing. This means that the airflow over the wing is hardly affected. Engineers can take off the engine casings easily for maintenance.

ACTION AND REACTION

The jet engine mixes air with a spray of fuel, and burns these to make a continuous blast of hot gases which rush out of the back. The engine reacts by being pushed forwards. This reaction is called 'thrust'.

In a turbofan some air enters the main engine, or engine core, for mixing with the fuel. But up to ten times as much air flows around the engine core, inside the outer casing. This helps to cool and quieten the jet, and to give extra thrust.

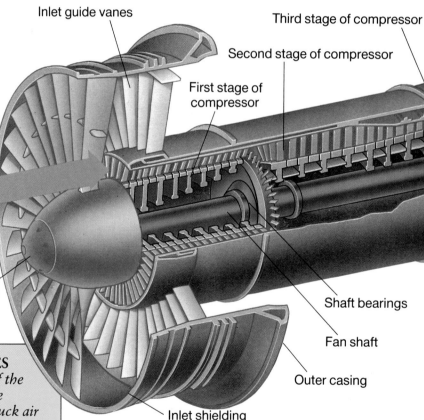

Inlet guide vanes

Third stage of compressor

Second stage of compressor

First stage of compressor

Nose cone

Shaft bearings

Fan shaft

Outer casing

Inlet shielding

Blade

FAN BLADES
The blades of the intake fan are designed to suck air in and push it backwards, around and through the engine. The blades come in pairs, so if one cracks, both it and its opposite partner must be replaced. Most fan blades are made of titanium, an expensive metal that is light and strong.

Blade root

Hub

Linking shroud

THE FAN
The giant fan at the front of a turbofan engine is called the **intake fan**. It is mounted on a shaft that runs the length of the engine. The shaft is spun around by the hot gases rushing through the **turbine** at the rear of the jet engine. The intake fan pushes air backwards into the engine.

THE COMPRESSOR
The **compressor** is made up of fans with many blades, mounted on the shaft. The blades of the compressor squeeze, or compress, the incoming air, stage by stage, until it is under tremendous pressure. The air is then mixed with the fuel in the next part of the engine, the combustion chamber.

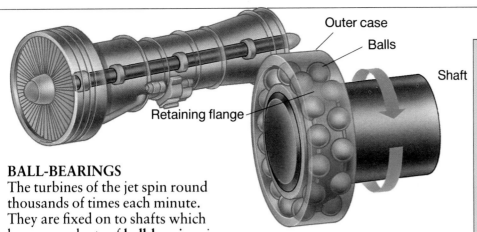

Outer case
Balls
Shaft
Retaining flange

BALL-BEARINGS

The turbines of the jet spin round thousands of times each minute. They are fixed on to shafts which have several sets of **ball-bearings** in between them. These ball-bearings are specially designed to withstand the enormous temperatures inside the engine core.

Low pressure turbines
High pressure turbines
Heat-resistant turbine blades
Combustion chamber

Exhaust gases

Inner (engine core) casing
Compressor shaft

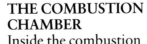

THE TURBINE

As the hot gases roar out from the combustion chamber, they make the fan-shaped turbines spin round. The turbines are linked by a shaft to turn the blades in the compressor, and to spin the intake fan at the front.

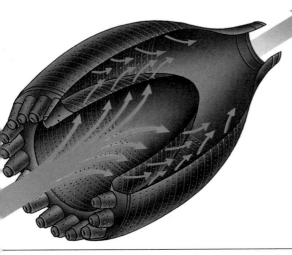

THE COMBUSTION CHAMBER

Inside the combustion chamber, about 20 nozzles spray fuel into the airstream. The resulting mixture catches fire at almost 2,700°F. The chamber is lined with heat-resistant **ceramic** materials.

TYPES OF JET

The thrust of a turbojet comes from hot exhaust gases. In the turboprop, the turbine is connected to a propeller in front of the engine. The ramjet has neither compressor nor turbine. It relies on fast-moving air for combustion.

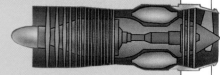

The turbojet does not have a front fan.

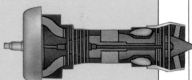

The ramjet slows fast-moving air for combustion.

The turboprop has a propeller connected to its turbine.

ROCKET PLANES

A rocket engine works in a similar way to a jet engine, setting fire to the fuel in a non-stop explosion. But the rocket has no turbines and does not need oxygen-containing air for combustion. It carries its own supply of oxygen, as part of the fuel.

The X-15 rocket plane

Steering through the sky

The first plane-makers tried various layouts for wings and tails. Most airplanes today have three surfaces at the rear end of the fuselage, to keep the plane moving in a straight line. Two of these are horizontal stabilizers, that stop the rear end from flapping up and down. They are like miniature versions of the main wings, and are called **tailplanes**. The third is the vertical stabilizer or fin, which prevents the fuselage twisting left and right. The tailplanes and fin have moveable control surfaces for steering the aircraft.

STREAMLINED DESIGN

The tailplanes and fin have a swept-back design, like the main wings. This streamlined design helps to reduce friction with the air (friction produces a slowing-down force known as '**drag**').

THE INSIDE STRUCTURE

The tailplanes and fin have an inner framework of spars and ribs, covered with a skin of metal sheets. As in the main wing, the skin is not only a covering. It is also an essential part of the strength and stiffness of the whole structure.

Hinge damper

Rudder movements

Elevator movements

CONTROL SURFACES

The elevators are so-called because when they are tilted up, the air rushing over them pushes the rear of the plane down. This makes the front of the plane tilt up, or elevate, and so the plane climbs. The rudder works like the rudder of a ship. If it sticks out to the left, the airflow swings the rear of the plane to the right, and so the plane turns left.

in neutral

Airflow with elevators in neutral

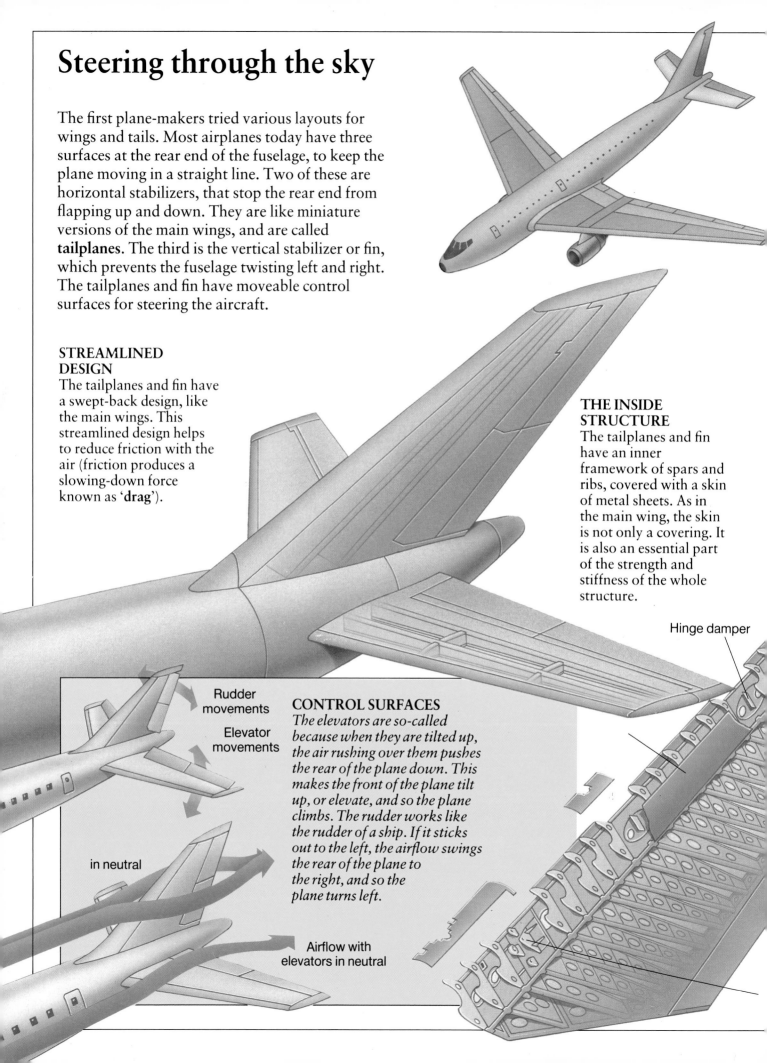

THE RUDDER

In many aircraft, the rudder forms half or more of the whole surface of the fin. It is linked to the fin by a series of pivot joints. Its movements are controlled so that it does not flap as the plane changes speed. Rudder movements are usually controlled by the pilot's foot pedals.

Rudder tip

Flashing beacon

Rear spar

Front spar

Rib

THE ELEVATOR

The elevator is hinged to the main rear spar in the tailplane, The elevator itself may have smaller elevator-type surfaces on it, called trim tabs. These are adjusted for every individual plane so that, with the controls in neutral, the plane will fly straight and level. A forward projection at the tip of the elevator, the balance horn, acts as a counterbalance to the weight of the elevator, making it easier to move.

Trailing edge

Skin

Hinge

Rib

Hinge and damper

Trailing edge

Front spar

Leading edge

Balance horn

REAR ENDS

To make the airflow over the main wings as smooth as possible, some plane designers have put the engines at the rear of the fuselage. This means building them into the tailplane, or sitting the tailplane on top of the fin.

Vickers VC10 has four engines in two pairs on horizontal pylons

Lockheed Tri-Star has three engines,

Some planes have two engines, one under each tailplane.

WIDE LOADS

Some cargo planes have huge doors in the rear of the fuselage. Trucks and even tanks can be driven up ramps, straight into the plane. Planes such as these are used to deliver vital foods and medicines to remote areas in times of war or famine.

The fuselage

The fuselage is the central 'body' of the airplane. The wings, tailplanes, fin and engines are all attached to it. In a modern passenger airplane, flying off to a vacation in the sun, you are seated only in the top half of the fuselage. The floor of the passenger cabin runs along most of the length of the fuselage. Under your feet is a similar sized space for luggage, freight, fuel, control cables, pipes and wires, girders and **struts**, and other equipment.

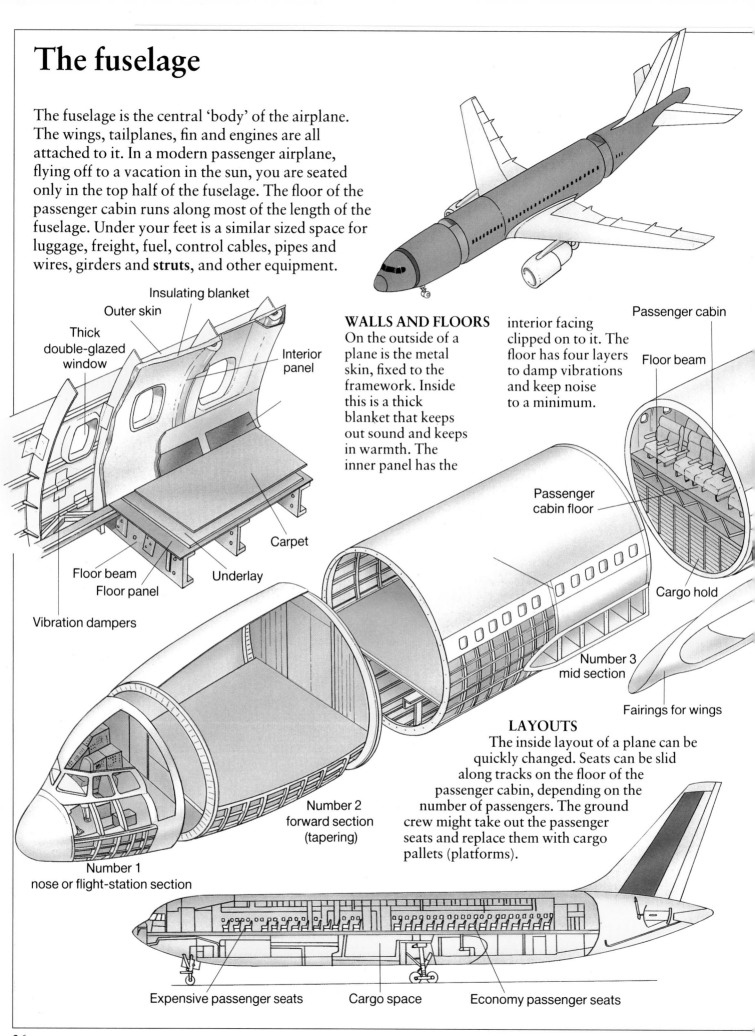

Insulating blanket

Outer skin

Thick double-glazed window

Interior panel

Carpet

Underlay

Floor beam

Floor panel

Vibration dampers

WALLS AND FLOORS
On the outside of a plane is the metal skin, fixed to the framework. Inside this is a thick blanket that keeps out sound and keeps in warmth. The inner panel has the interior facing clipped on to it. The floor has four layers to damp vibrations and keep noise to a minimum.

Passenger cabin

Floor beam

Passenger cabin floor

Cargo hold

Number 3 mid section

Fairings for wings

Number 2 forward section (tapering)

Number 1 nose or flight-station section

LAYOUTS
The inside layout of a plane can be quickly changed. Seats can be slid along tracks on the floor of the passenger cabin, depending on the number of passengers. The ground crew might take out the passenger seats and replace them with cargo pallets (platforms).

Expensive passenger seats

Cargo space

Economy passenger seats

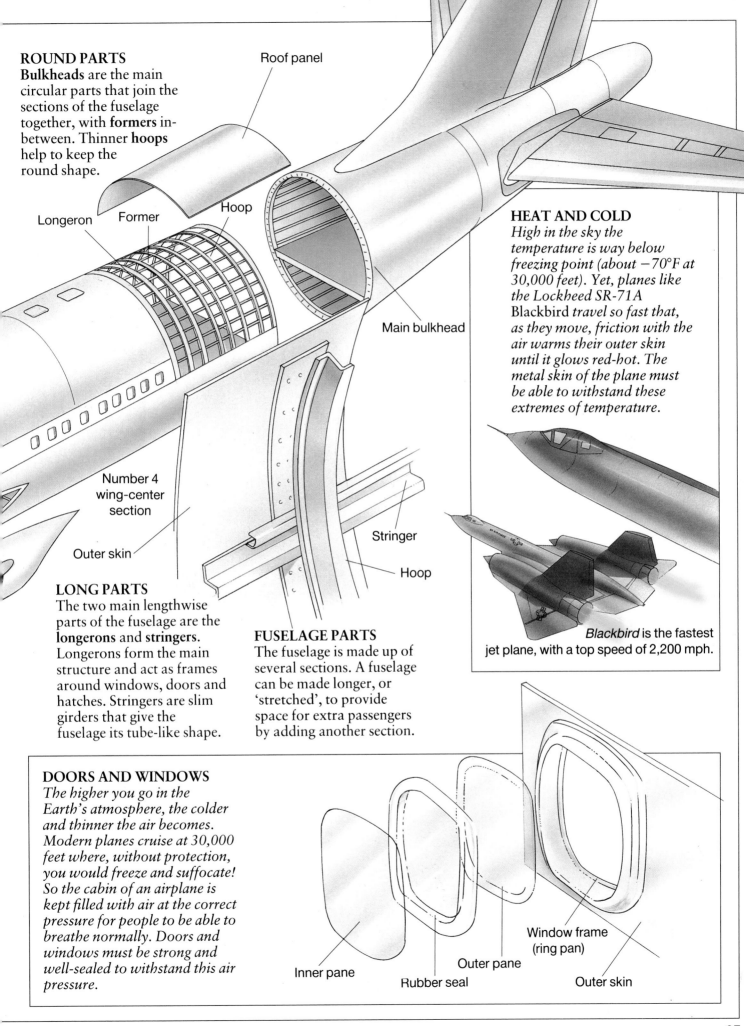

ROUND PARTS

Bulkheads are the main circular parts that join the sections of the fuselage together, with **formers** in-between. Thinner **hoops** help to keep the round shape.

Roof panel

Longeron Former Hoop

Main bulkhead

Number 4 wing-center section

Outer skin

Stringer

Hoop

LONG PARTS

The two main lengthwise parts of the fuselage are the **longerons** and **stringers**. Longerons form the main structure and act as frames around windows, doors and hatches. Stringers are slim girders that give the fuselage its tube-like shape.

FUSELAGE PARTS

The fuselage is made up of several sections. A fuselage can be made longer, or 'stretched', to provide space for extra passengers by adding another section.

HEAT AND COLD

High in the sky the temperature is way below freezing point (about −70°F at 30,000 feet). Yet, planes like the Lockheed SR-71A Blackbird travel so fast that, as they move, friction with the air warms their outer skin until it glows red-hot. The metal skin of the plane must be able to withstand these extremes of temperature.

Blackbird is the fastest jet plane, with a top speed of 2,200 mph.

DOORS AND WINDOWS

The higher you go in the Earth's atmosphere, the colder and thinner the air becomes. Modern planes cruise at 30,000 feet where, without protection, you would freeze and suffocate! So the cabin of an airplane is kept filled with air at the correct pressure for people to be able to breathe normally. Doors and windows must be strong and well-sealed to withstand this air pressure.

Inner pane

Rubber seal

Outer pane

Window frame (ring pan)

Outer skin

Finding your way

Flying far above the Earth's surface, it is easy to see landmarks such as towns and airports – except when it is hazy, foggy, cloudy, raining or dark! The **radar** systems in modern planes use radio waves to find the way, or navigate, even in thick clouds and at night. Gyroscopes and other equipment detect changes in the plane's flight path, as it turns or alters height. And the newest computer-controlled 'automatic pilots' can fly and land a plane almost on their own, while the pilot watches for problems.

PLANE SENSORS

A jetliner has several sensors that detect its movements. There are usually three or more gyroscopes, with heavy, fast-spinning wheels. As the plane banks and turns, climbs and dives, the spinning wheel stays in a steady position. But the frame of the gyroscope moves with the plane. The alteration is detected by electrical sensors and fed to the pilot's instruments and computers. There are also accelerometers, which measure how fast the plane is speeding up or slowing down.

THE GYROSCOPE

In a gyroscope, the joints between the heavy spinning wheel and its outer ring are almost friction-free. This allows the spinning wheel to stay steady as the outer ring moves with the plane.

Outer gimbal ring
Inner gimbal ring
Spinning wheel
Low-friction bearings
Steady flight
Wheel and rings in line

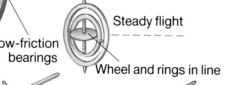

Banked turn
Rings tilt
Wheel stays horizontal

SIDE WINDS
As the plane flies along, a wind blowing from the side will push it sideways. The pilot steers into the wind, to keep the correct ground course.

Wind direction

AUTOPILOT PARTS
The autopilot makes use of the plane's movement sensors, navigation instruments and computer in order to operate the controls.

Autopilot computer
Connecting wires
Gyroscopes and accelerometers
Weather radar

CLIMB OR DIVE
The autopilot receives information from the altimeter about the plane's height. When the pilot sets a new height the plane goes up or down automatically.

BACK TO MANUAL
While the autopilot is turned on, the pilot's controls move as though pushed by invisible hands. But at the flick of a switch, the pilot can change from auto and take manual control again.

ON COURSE
The autopilot also receives information from radar beacons on the ground, through the airplane's radar equipment. It can change course to keep on the radar path.

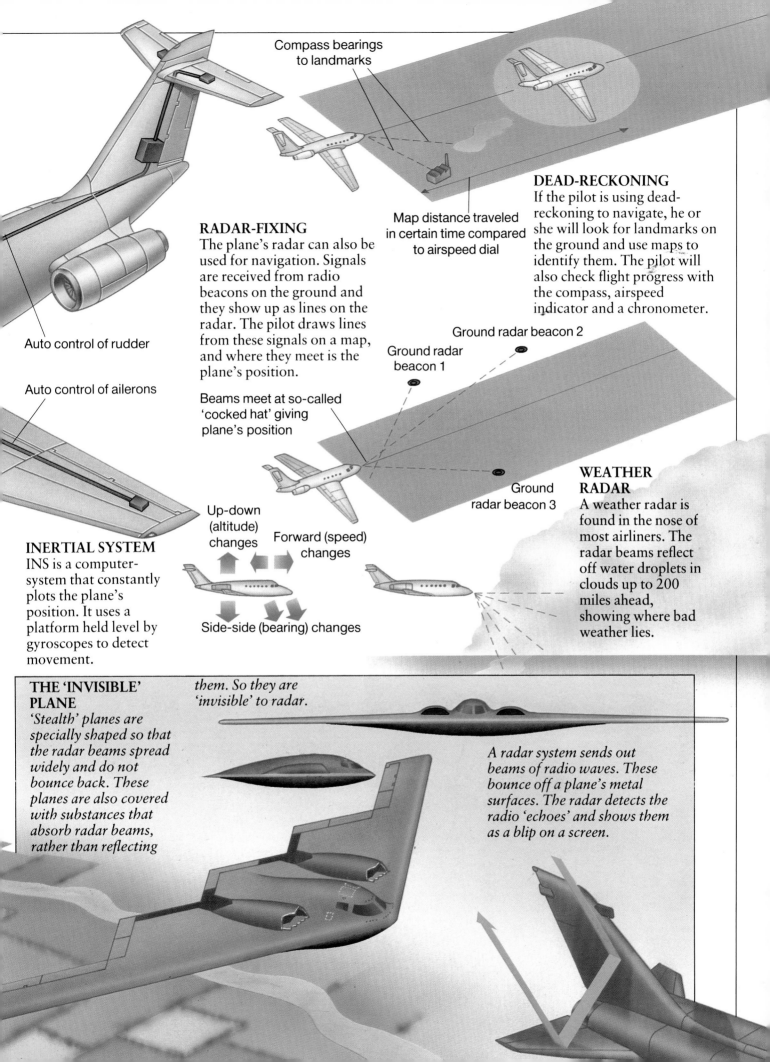

Compass bearings to landmarks

Auto control of rudder

Auto control of ailerons

RADAR-FIXING

The plane's radar can also be used for navigation. Signals are received from radio beacons on the ground and they show up as lines on the radar. The pilot draws lines from these signals on a map, and where they meet is the plane's position.

Beams meet at so-called 'cocked hat' giving plane's position

Map distance traveled in certain time compared to airspeed dial

DEAD-RECKONING

If the pilot is using dead-reckoning to navigate, he or she will look for landmarks on the ground and use maps to identify them. The pilot will also check flight progress with the compass, airspeed indicator and a chronometer.

Ground radar beacon 2

Ground radar beacon 1

Ground radar beacon 3

INERTIAL SYSTEM

INS is a computer-system that constantly plots the plane's position. It uses a platform held level by gyroscopes to detect movement.

Up-down (altitude) changes

Forward (speed) changes

Side-side (bearing) changes

WEATHER RADAR

A weather radar is found in the nose of most airliners. The radar beams reflect off water droplets in clouds up to 200 miles ahead, showing where bad weather lies.

THE 'INVISIBLE' PLANE

'Stealth' planes are specially shaped so that the radar beams spread widely and do not bounce back. These planes are also covered with substances that absorb radar beams, rather than reflecting them. So they are 'invisible' to radar.

A radar system sends out beams of radio waves. These bounce off a plane's metal surfaces. The radar detects the radio 'echoes' and shows them as a blip on a screen.

Landing gear

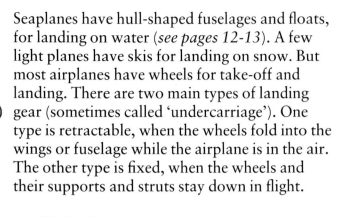

Lock-down indicator

Wing support

Support bracket

Drag Strut

Side strut

Shock or main strut

Torque arm

Axle

Bogie beam   Tire

Seaplanes have hull-shaped fuselages and floats, for landing on water (*see pages 12-13*). A few light planes have skis for landing on snow. But most airplanes have wheels for take-off and landing. There are two main types of landing gear (sometimes called 'undercarriage'). One type is retractable, when the wheels fold into the wings or fuselage while the airplane is in the air. The other type is fixed, when the wheels and their supports and struts stay down in flight.

MAIN GEAR

Many big planes have a three part 'tricycle' landing gear. The nose gear is the small set of wheels at the front of the plane. The other two sets of main gears (*left*) are underneath the wing roots.

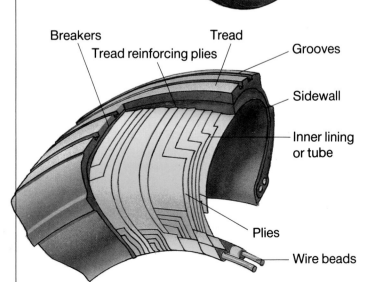

Breakers   Tread

Tread reinforcing plies

Grooves

Sidewall

Inner lining or tube

Plies

Wire beads

TIRES

The tires of a jumbo jet are almost as tall as an adult person. They are made of layers, or plies, of rubber-coated nylon material, fixed to wire rings called beads. The outer surface of the tire is the tread, which grips the runway. The grooves of the tread fling away water, and make braking effective even when the runway is wet.

UP AND AWAY

Fixed landing gear spoils the plane's streamlining and slows it down. This means slower journeys and wasted fuel. So the landing gear of a passenger jet folds into its fuselage and wings soon after take-off, and unfolds again just before landing.

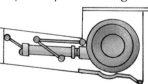

Gear folds into bin (compartment) in flight

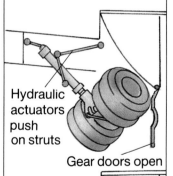

Hydraulic actuators push on struts

Gear doors open

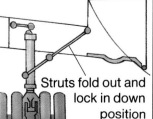

Struts fold out and lock in down position

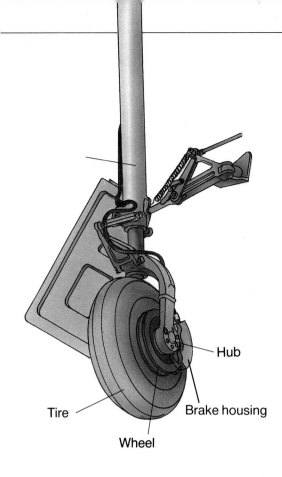

LIGHT PLANE WHEEL

The landing gear of a light plane has many similarities to a car wheel. Inside the hub, the wheel revolves on two sets of ball-bearings. The nose wheel is steered by the pilot pressing the rudder pedals as the plane taxis along the ground.

HOLDING

At a busy airport there may be several planes lining up to land. They take instructions from the control tower, and each plane flies around a long level circuit at a certain height as it waits.

Hub

Tire

Brake housing

Wheel

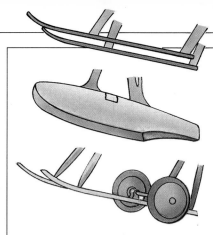

SKIDS, FLOATS AND SKIS

Some light planes can be fitted with wheels for runways, skis for snow, skids for ice, or floats for water, depending on the conditions. This is useful in cold regions with lakes that freeze over in winter.

BRAKES

Almost all planes have brakes on their wheels, usually disc brakes. Brake pads are fixed to the hub of the wheel. They press on the rotating metal disc which is attached to the wheel, and slow it down. Big jetliners have five or more discs in each wheel.

LANDING

When instructed, the plane descends 1,000 feet to the next level, and so on. This is called 'stacking'. Eventually the pilot hears: "You are cleared for landing".

Flight-deck instruments use radar beams to show if the plane is on the correct approach, or landing path.

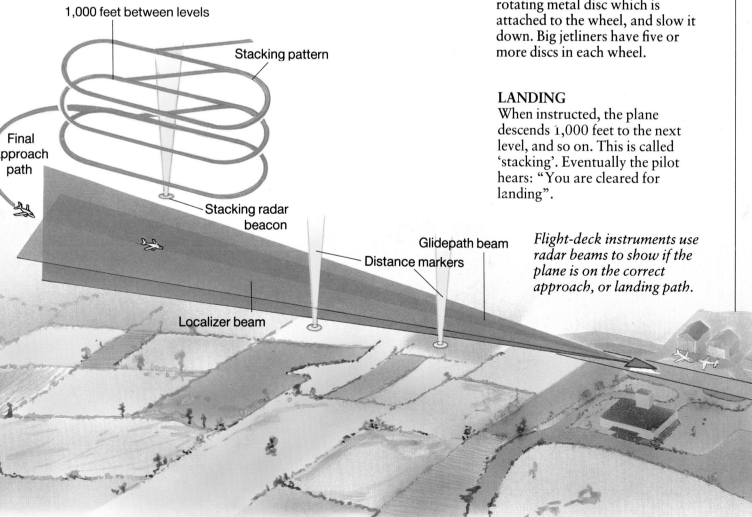

1,000 feet between levels

Stacking pattern

Final approach path

Stacking radar beacon

Glidepath beam

Distance markers

Localizer beam

Pilots in control

Like the steering wheel and dashboard of a car, the flight deck is the control center of an airplane. A modern jetliner has a flickering array of gadgets. TV monitor screens, dials, gauges, warning lights, radar displays and other instruments tell the pilots what is happening both inside and outside the plane. The pilot controls the plane and all its various systems, from the engine speed to the temperature inside the passengers' toilets.

A PILOT'S-EYE VIEW
On the flight deck of a big passenger jet there are two complete sets of controls. So if one control should fail there is always a back-up. The captain sits on the left and is in charge. The first officer sits on the right. The banks of switches and levers between them control the engines. The latest flight decks have computer screens to replace some of the dials and lights. These can show information more clearly, and flash up warnings if there is an emergency.

Even a small light plane (*above*) has an impressive set of dials and other instruments. The most important instruments are the same as on a jetliner.

Light plane controls

Passenger plane controls

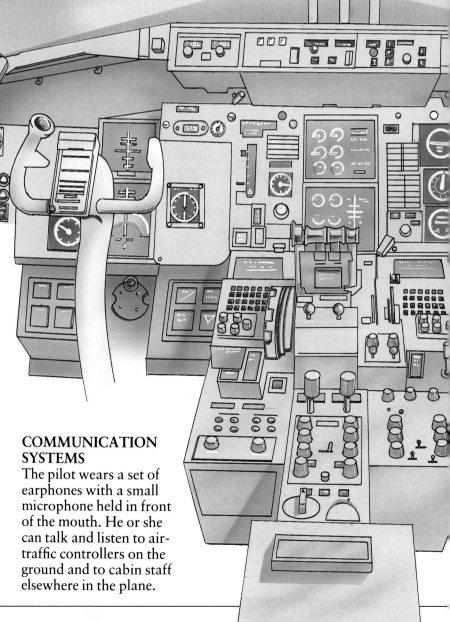

HOW HIGH?
The altimeter measures an airplane's height (altitude). The simplest designs work by using air pressure, which becomes less as you go higher. Air sealed into a container with a thin metal wall expands as the plane rises.

The expanding capsule is linked by levers and gears to the dial.

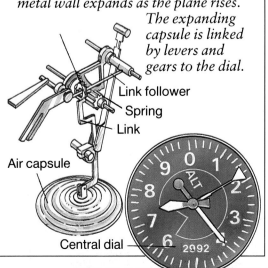

Link follower
Spring
Link
Air capsule
Central dial

COMMUNICATION SYSTEMS
The pilot wears a set of earphones with a small microphone held in front of the mouth. He or she can talk and listen to air-traffic controllers on the ground and to cabin staff elsewhere in the plane.

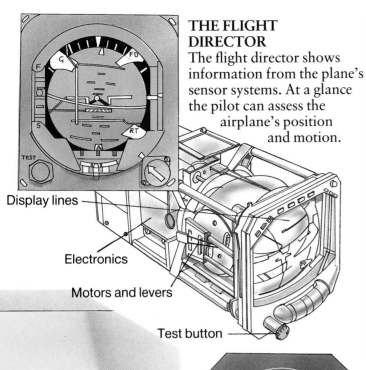

THE FLIGHT DIRECTOR

The flight director shows information from the plane's sensor systems. At a glance the pilot can assess the airplane's position and motion.

Display lines

Electronics

Motors and levers

Test button

THE 'BLACK BOX'

The 'black box' is the nickname for the flight data recorder. It records information about the flight. If the plane should crash, the 'black box' could provide vital clues about what went wrong.

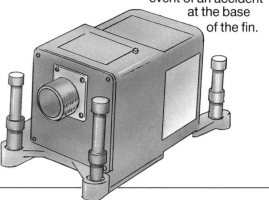

The recorder is sited where damage is least likely in the event of an accident at the base of the fin.

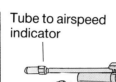

Tube to airspeed indicator

Static pressure tube

THE PITOT HEAD

The pitot head is a small tube which is usually mounted on the plane's fin, wing or nose. The rate of the air rushing into it is measured to give the airspeed. Tubes link it to instruments such as the altimeter and vertical-speed indicator.

HOW FAST?

The airspeed dial shows how fast the plane is flying through the air. This may be different from the groundspeed, which is the speed at which the plane is traveling in relation to the ground. For example, a plane with an airspeed of 300 mph flying directly into a wind of 100 mph has a groundspeed of only 200 mph.

HEAD-UP DISPLAY

A fast jet fighter can travel a mile in the time it takes for the pilot to glance down at the instruments. The head-up display reflects the instruments off a screeen or helmet visor, into the pilot's line of vision. The pilot can see the instruments, and beyond them the view outside the plane, without having to look down.

Pilot's line of vision   Semi-reflecting glass

Light from outside view

Light from instruments

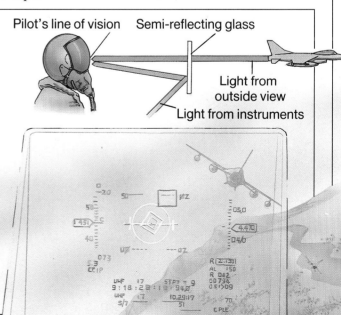

WHICH WAY?

The direction indicator is based on a gyroscope (*see page 28*). It shows the pilot which way the plane is pointing compared to North. The device is regularly checked and adjusted according to the magnetic compass.

Fighters and bombers

Modern wars are fought largely in the skies. Fast fighter and bomber planes carry guns, missiles and bombs. They skim just above the ground, in order to stay undetected by the enemy's radar beams. High in the sky, large planes with sensitive antennae (aerials) act as flying radio and radar stations. They give early warning of the enemy's actions. They also pass on information and commands by radio to other aircraft, warships and army units.

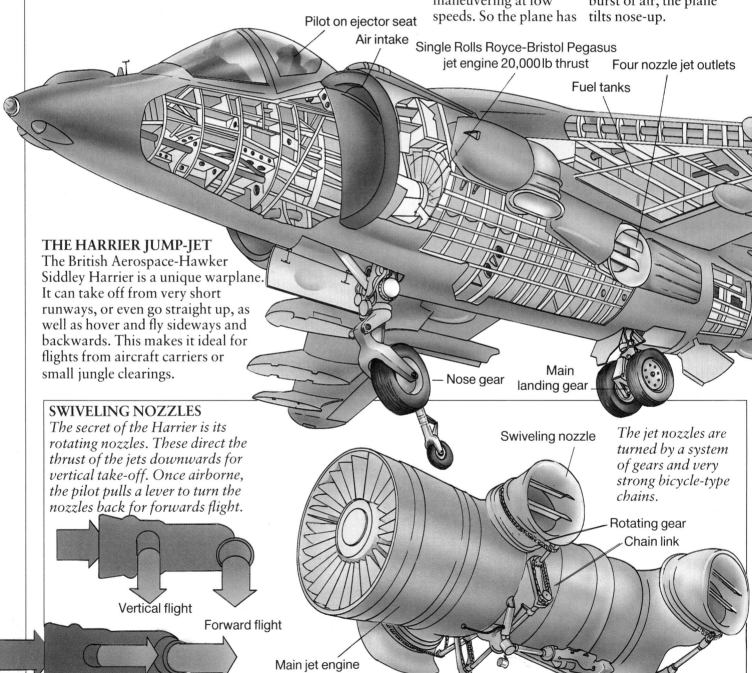

REACTION JETS
The Harrier's main jet nozzles (*see below*) are too powerful and not adjustable enough for fine control and maneuvering at low speeds. So the plane has small compressed-air 'puffers', called reaction jets, in its nose, wing tips and tail. If the nose reaction jet sends out a burst of air, the plane tilts nose-up.

Pilot on ejector seat

Air intake

Single Rolls Royce-Bristol Pegasus jet engine 20,000 lb thrust

Four nozzle jet outlets

Fuel tanks

THE HARRIER JUMP-JET
The British Aerospace-Hawker Siddley Harrier is a unique warplane. It can take off from very short runways, or even go straight up, as well as hover and fly sideways and backwards. This makes it ideal for flights from aircraft carriers or small jungle clearings.

Nose gear

Main landing gear

SWIVELING NOZZLES
The secret of the Harrier is its rotating nozzles. These direct the thrust of the jets downwards for vertical take-off. Once airborne, the pilot pulls a lever to turn the nozzles back for forwards flight.

Swiveling nozzle

The jet nozzles are turned by a system of gears and very strong bicycle-type chains.

Rotating gear

Chain link

Vertical flight

Forward flight

Main jet engine

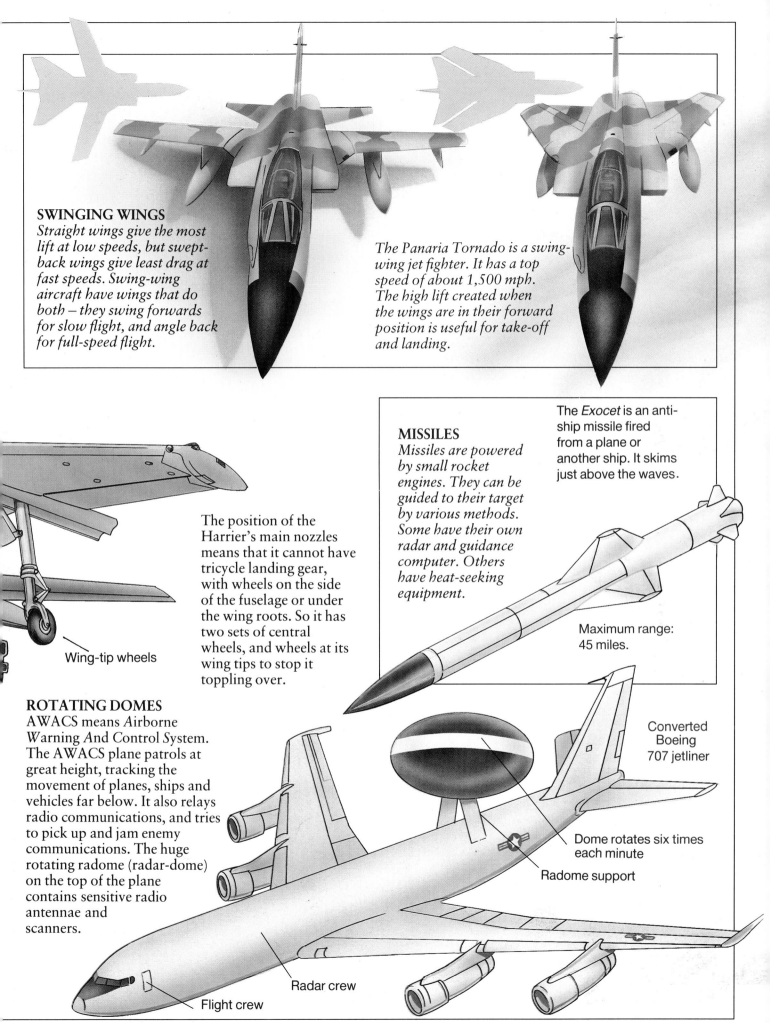

SWINGING WINGS

Straight wings give the most lift at low speeds, but swept-back wings give least drag at fast speeds. Swing-wing aircraft have wings that do both — they swing forwards for slow flight, and angle back for full-speed flight.

The Panaria Tornado is a swing-wing jet fighter. It has a top speed of about 1,500 mph. The high lift created when the wings are in their forward position is useful for take-off and landing.

Wing-tip wheels

The position of the Harrier's main nozzles means that it cannot have tricycle landing gear, with wheels on the side of the fuselage or under the wing roots. So it has two sets of central wheels, and wheels at its wing tips to stop it toppling over.

MISSILES

Missiles are powered by small rocket engines. They can be guided to their target by various methods. Some have their own radar and guidance computer. Others have heat-seeking equipment.

The *Exocet* is an anti-ship missile fired from a plane or another ship. It skims just above the waves.

Maximum range: 45 miles.

ROTATING DOMES

AWACS means *Airborne Warning And Control System*. The AWACS plane patrols at great height, tracking the movement of planes, ships and vehicles far below. It also relays radio communications, and tries to pick up and jam enemy communications. The huge rotating radome (radar-dome) on the top of the plane contains sensitive radio antennae and scanners.

Converted Boeing 707 jetliner

Dome rotates six times each minute

Radome support

Radar crew

Flight crew

Helicopters

A normal airplane gets lift from its wings as it moves forwards through the air. A helicopter has very long, thin wings, known as rotor blades, that whirl around above its main cabin. As the blades rotate they push air downwards, creating lift. A helicopter can hover over one spot; it can even move backwards! Helicopters are known as 'rotary-wing' craft, and their engines, cabins and controls are quite different from the ordinary 'fixed-wing' plane.

INSIDE THE ROTOR HEAD
When the pilot moves the joystick in the cabin, his or her movements are transferred to the spinning rotors above by an adjustable connection called a swashplate coupling. The circular swashplate is attached to connecting rods that change the angle of the rotor blades. The swashplate can tilt, giving extra lift to the rotors in part of their circle. This makes the helicopter move in the direction of the tilt.

SAR (Search And Rescue) helicopters have a winch and line, which runs over a pulley above the side of the main cabin door. The winch is operated by a powerful electrical motor.

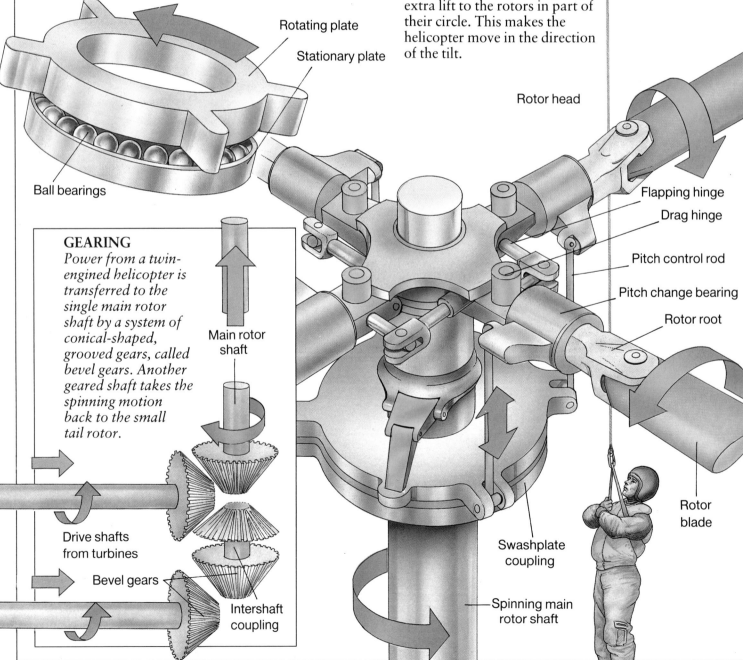

Swashplate coupling

Rotating plate

Stationary plate

Ball bearings

Rotor head

Flapping hinge

Drag hinge

Pitch control rod

Pitch change bearing

Rotor root

GEARING
Power from a twin-engined helicopter is transferred to the single main rotor shaft by a system of conical-shaped, grooved gears, called bevel gears. Another geared shaft takes the spinning motion back to the small tail rotor.

Main rotor shaft

Drive shafts from turbines

Bevel gears

Intershaft coupling

Swashplate coupling

Spinning main rotor shaft

Rotor blade

INSIDE THE ROTOR BLADE

Modern rotor blades are made of metal alloys and carbon-fiber materials. They are designed to give strength exactly where it is needed, and to be light and flexible. The rotor blade is an airfoil shape, like a plane wing.

THE GAS TURBINE

A gas turbine provides the power for modern helicopters. It works in a similar way to the turbojet (*see pages 22-3*). The blades of the turbine spin round thousands of times every second, and their tips travel at more than 65,000 mph. They are made of light, strong materials, such as titanium alloys.

Individual turbine blades

Exhaust cone

Exhaust nozzle

Combustion chamber

Fuel igniter

Compressor turbine

Intake chamber

Spinning turbine (rotor)

Air intake

UP AND DOWN

The angle of the rotor blade is called its pitch. When angled up, at high pitch, it creates more lift. Coupled with a fast engine speed making the blades spin fast, this makes the helicopter rise. Lower pitches give less lift, to make the helicopter hover or move downwards.

High pitch and fast engine speed
Helicopter rises

Medium pitch and medium engine speed
Helicopter hovers

Low pitch and low engine speed
Helicopter descends

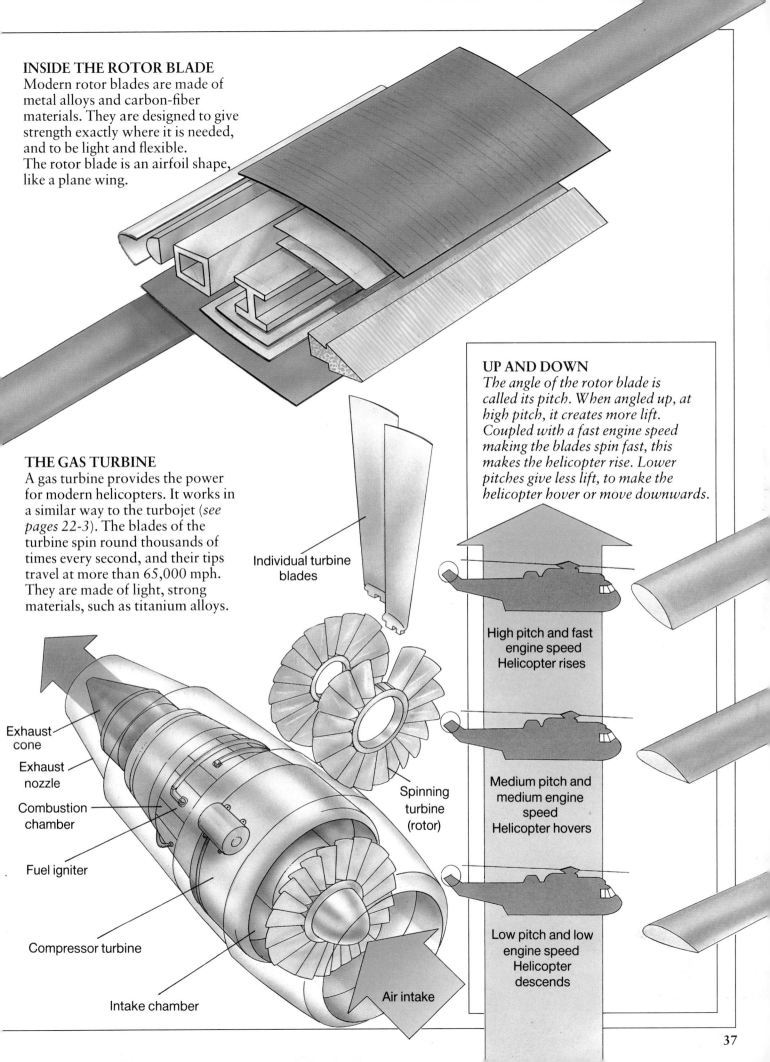

Soaring in silence

In 1804, the English inventor George Cayley made a model glider with a rudder and elevators. These could be adjusted so that the glider turned left or right, and descended at different speeds. This was one of the first examples of controlled gliding flight. Today's sailplanes use the same principles. A sailplane can never 'glide up'. But if the pilot can find a column of naturally warm rising air – called a 'thermal' – he or she can circle in it to gain height, and soar silently for hours.

Engine produces about 50 horsepower

Engine is retractable (withdraws into fuselage)

Overall weight around 1,000 lb

Take-off needs about 1,300 feet of runway

A POWERED GLIDER
A motorized glider may seem like a contradiction. But the engine is used only for take-off and emergencies. The rest of the time, the aircraft is a sailplane. Motor-gliders are a relatively new type of craft. The first International Motor Gliding Competition was held in Germany in 1974.

Lightweight plastic skin

Air-brake (spoiler)

Very long, thin wings

SAVING WEIGHT
The modern glider is a marvel of lightweight construction. It uses a variety of very light aluminium alloys (combinations of metals), plastics, and the latest carbon-fiber materials. In this design the big, heavy wing spars are replaced by several much slimmer longerons. The total weight may be less than 1,000 pounds, including the pilot!

Fuselage

Mid-wing design

Headrest

Seat

Clear plastic cockpit cover

Control column

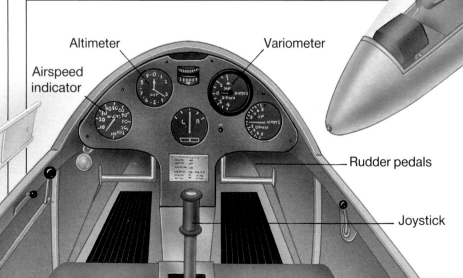

Altimeter

Variometer

Airspeed indicator

Rudder pedals

Joystick

IN THE COCKPIT
The main instruments of a glider are similar to those of any other aircraft, except, of course, there are no fuel gauges or engine throttles. One important dial is the variometer. This works like the airspeed indicator, but it shows speed downwards through the air, not forwards. It gives the pilot information about the glider's rate of descent, compared to the air around it.

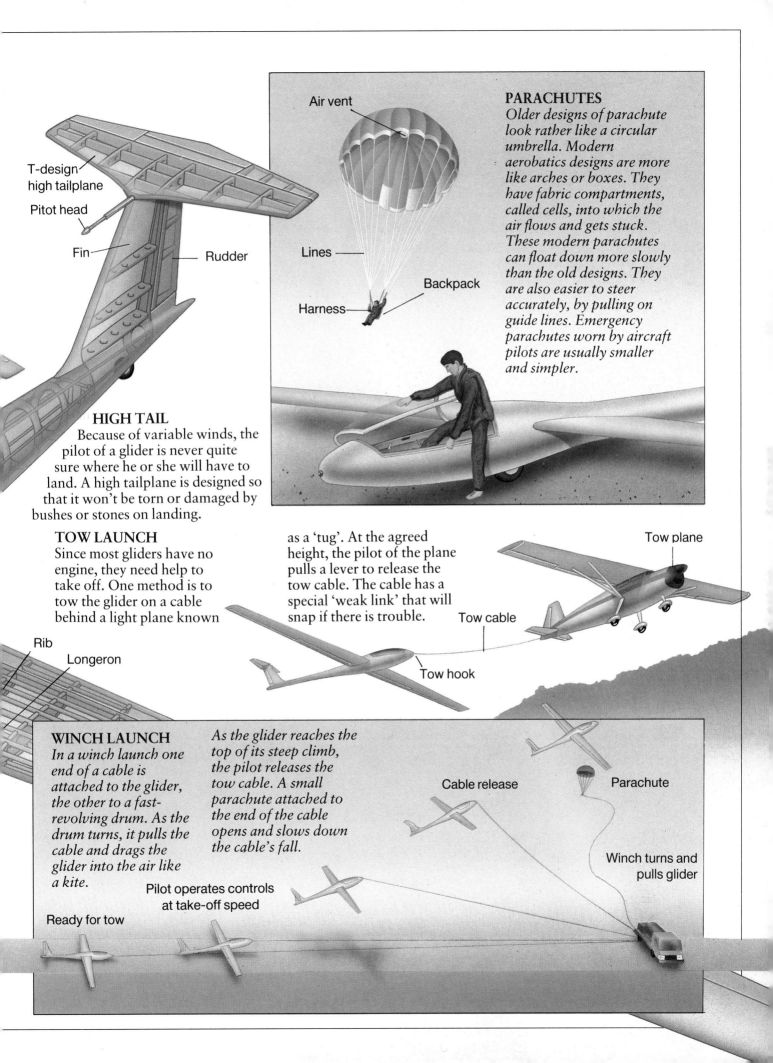

T-design
high tailplane

Pitot head

Fin

Rudder

HIGH TAIL

Because of variable winds, the pilot of a glider is never quite sure where he or she will have to land. A high tailplane is designed so that it won't be torn or damaged by bushes or stones on landing.

Air vent

Lines

Harness

Backpack

PARACHUTES

Older designs of parachute look rather like a circular umbrella. Modern aerobatics designs are more like arches or boxes. They have fabric compartments, called cells, into which the air flows and gets stuck. These modern parachutes can float down more slowly than the old designs. They are also easier to steer accurately, by pulling on guide lines. Emergency parachutes worn by aircraft pilots are usually smaller and simpler.

TOW LAUNCH

Since most gliders have no engine, they need help to take off. One method is to tow the glider on a cable behind a light plane known

as a 'tug'. At the agreed height, the pilot of the plane pulls a lever to release the tow cable. The cable has a special 'weak link' that will snap if there is trouble.

Tow plane

Tow cable

Tow hook

Rib

Longeron

WINCH LAUNCH

In a winch launch one end of a cable is attached to the glider, the other to a fast-revolving drum. As the drum turns, it pulls the cable and drags the glider into the air like a kite.

As the glider reaches the top of its steep climb, the pilot releases the tow cable. A small parachute attached to the end of the cable opens and slows down the cable's fall.

Cable release

Parachute

Pilot operates controls
at take-off speed

Ready for tow

Winch turns and
pulls glider

Microlights

The typical microlight is basically a hang-glider with an engine and a propeller attached. The shape of the modern hang-glider wing was developed mainly by an American professor, Francis Rogallo, during the 1950s. The Rogallo wing was designed to land space capsules safely back on Earth. Hanggliding became popular in the 1970s. Today, small motorcycle-type engines are fixed to hang-glider wings to make the simplest and least expensive powered craft in the air – microlights.

MICROLIGHT DESIGN
The wings of a microlight are made of a very light, rip-proof, synthetic (man-made) material such as Kevlar. This is stretched over a framework of ultra-light metal or carbon-composite tubes. Thin but strong nylon lines tie the parts together tautly.

EXPERIMENTS
Microlights are small and simple to make, so new designs can be tested relatively quickly and without too much expense. This version has an inverted (upside-down) vee-tail.

Guy lines

Wing panel

Main leading edge spar

Wing stiffening battens

Central spar

Steering frame

Fuel tank

Engine

Steering bar

TOW-ALONG PLANE
One great advantage of the microlight is that its wings can be detached, taken apart and rolled up, and the whole aircraft put on to a triangular trailer. This is pulled behind a car. So a microlight does not need a special aircraft hangar (shelter). It can be kept in a garage or small shed.

Propeller

WARNING SIGNS
The microlight's controls could hardly be simpler. The engine temperature gauge warns if the engine is getting too hot, and the fuel gauge shows when fuel is running low. Both warnings mean that a quick landing is necessary.

Wheel frame

Pilot's seat   Landing wheel

Altimeter

Wing-bag support

Rolled-up wings and spars in bag

Engine folds up

Tow bar

Trailer

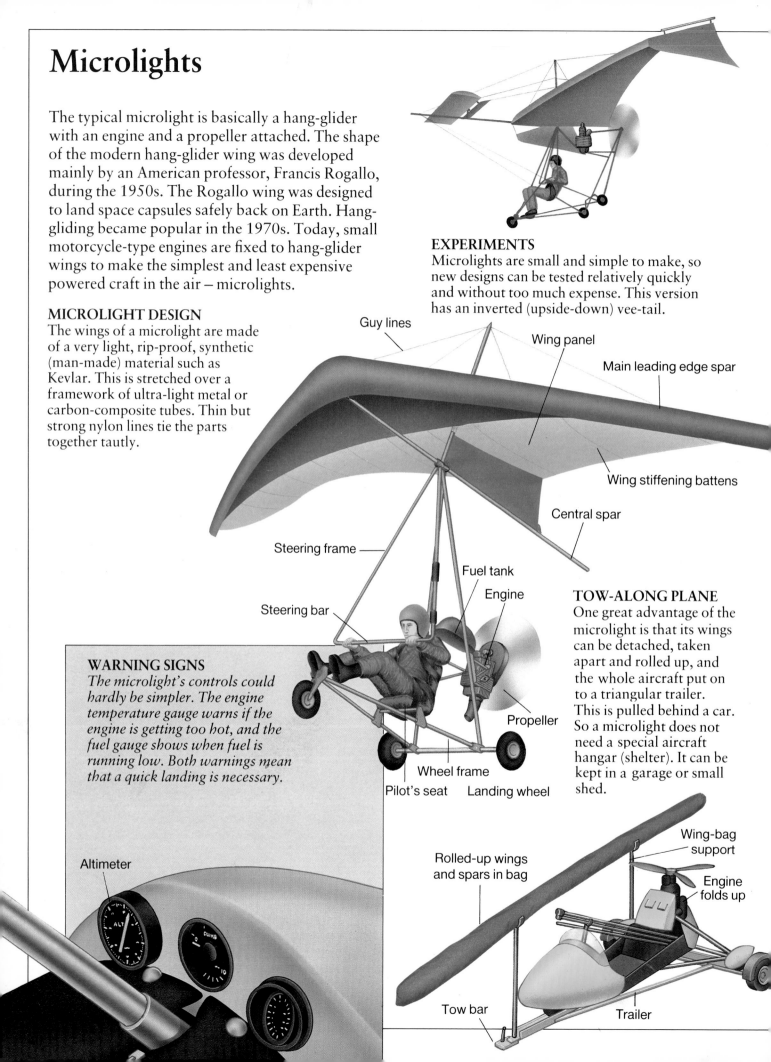

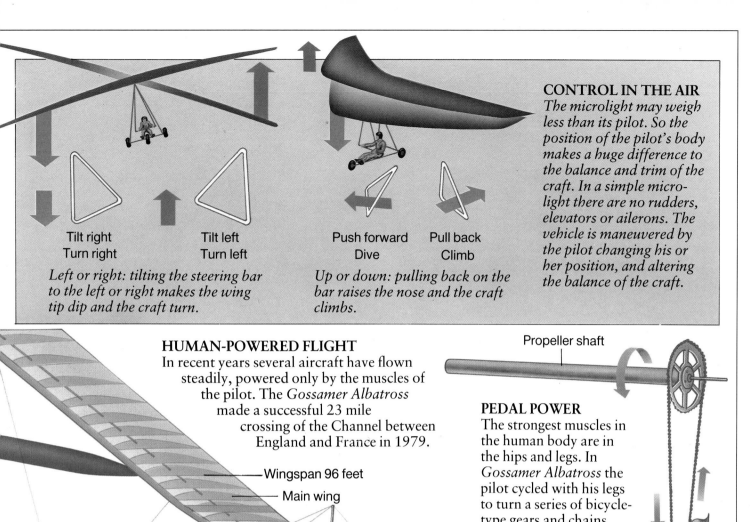

CONTROL IN THE AIR
The microlight may weigh less than its pilot. So the position of the pilot's body makes a huge difference to the balance and trim of the craft. In a simple microlight there are no rudders, elevators or ailerons. The vehicle is maneuvered by the pilot changing his or her position, and altering the balance of the craft.

Tilt right
Turn right

Tilt left
Turn left

Push forward
Dive

Pull back
Climb

Left or right: tilting the steering bar to the left or right makes the wing tip dip and the craft turn.

Up or down: pulling back on the bar raises the nose and the craft climbs.

HUMAN-POWERED FLIGHT
In recent years several aircraft have flown steadily, powered only by the muscles of the pilot. The *Gossamer Albatross* made a successful 23 mile crossing of the Channel between England and France in 1979.

Wingspan 96 feet

Main wing

PEDAL POWER
The strongest muscles in the human body are in the hips and legs. In *Gossamer Albatross* the pilot cycled with his legs to turn a series of bicycle-type gears and chains that were linked to the propeller shaft.

Propeller shaft

Pusher-propeller

Pilot's compartment

Seat

Lightweight frame

Canard wing

Mylar plastic sheet skin

Pedal

Crank

Cog

Cog

Spar

LIGHT AS A FEATHER
Specialist aircraft such as *Gossamer Albatross* are so light and fragile that they can easily blow over and snap. Incredibly light metal and plastic tubes are covered by a clingfilm-type skin.

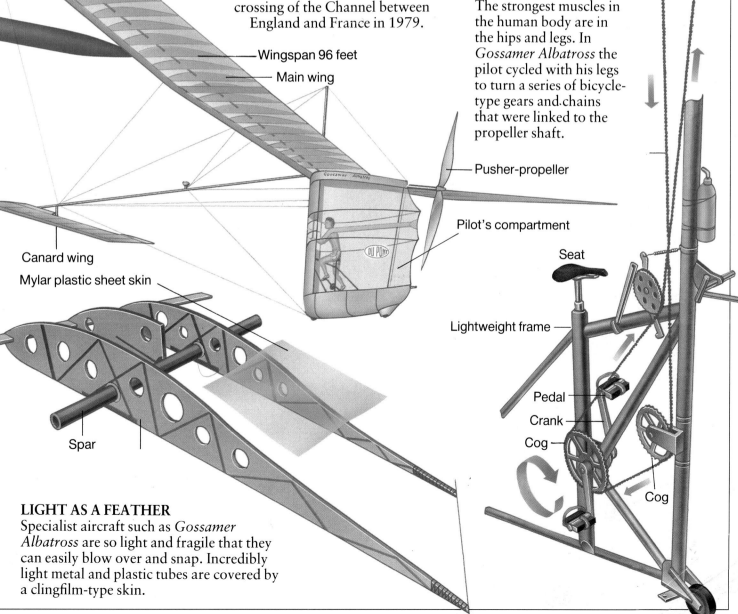

Lighter than air

Powered airplanes, helicopters, gliders and hang-gliders are all heavier than air. But balloons and airships float because the gas inside them is lighter, or less dense, than the surrounding air. During the 1920s-30s, massive airships droned across the world's skies, carrying passengers in great luxury. But the lighter-than-air hydrogen gas in their bags caught fire easily. A series of horrific fires and crashes brought the glorious airship era to an end by 1937.

Support pylon

Control rods and lines

Propeller

Diesel engine

ENGINES
In the past, airships had huge propeller-turning diesel engines, mounted on pylons to hold them clear of the gas bags. The Graf Zeppelin II's four diesel engines each produced 1000 horsepower.

STEERING
A typical airship has rudders and elevators mounted on the rear stabilizers or fins. They work like a plane's rudders and elevators.

Elevator up

Elevator down

Aluminium girder framework

Hoops

Longitudinal struts

Cross-braces

Gas cell

RIGID AND NON-RIGID
The type of airship with gas bags held in a stiff inner framework, like a series of cages, is known as a rigid airship or dirigible. The non-rigid airship, or blimp, is a series of strong bags joined together, with no frame. It only takes shape and becomes stiff when filled with gas, like blowing up a balloon.

Four 1050-horsepower Daimler Benz diesel engines

Total of 7 million cubic feet of hydrogen, enough to fill 250 average family houses

Internal walkways and steps

Control rooms

Passenger decks

QUEEN OF THE INTER-WAR SKIES
The great airships were nicknamed 'zeppelins' after Count Ferdinand Zeppelin, the German general who developed them. The longest was the *Hindenberg*, at 800 feet. It was launched in 1936, but crashed in flames the following year.

The *Hindenberg* was designed to carry 70 passengers and 45 crew across the Atlantic Ocean. It was the first passenger airliner in regular service between the US and Europe.

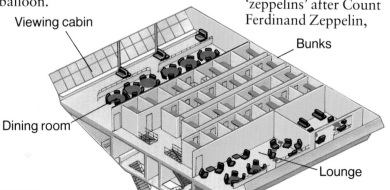

Viewing cabin

Dining room

Bunks

Lounge

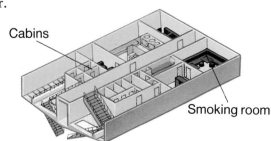

Cabins

Smoking room

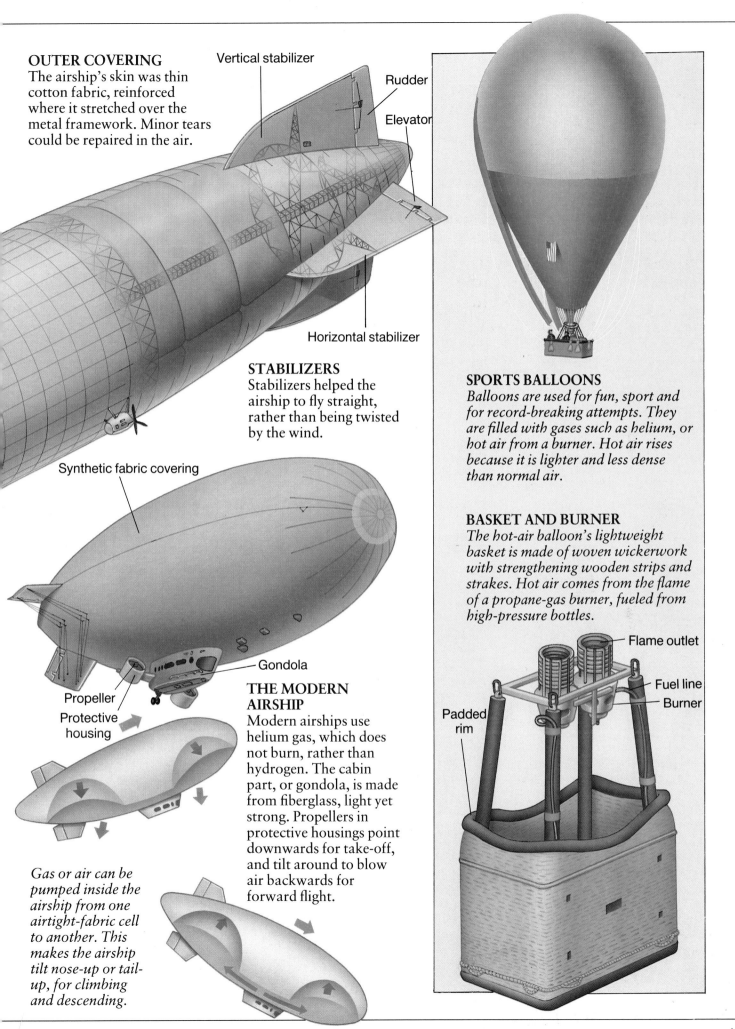

OUTER COVERING
The airship's skin was thin cotton fabric, reinforced where it stretched over the metal framework. Minor tears could be repaired in the air.

Vertical stabilizer

Rudder

Elevator

Horizontal stabilizer

STABILIZERS
Stabilizers helped the airship to fly straight, rather than being twisted by the wind.

Synthetic fabric covering

Gondola

Propeller

Protective housing

THE MODERN AIRSHIP
Modern airships use helium gas, which does not burn, rather than hydrogen. The cabin part, or gondola, is made from fiberglass, light yet strong. Propellers in protective housings point downwards for take-off, and tilt around to blow air backwards for forward flight.

Gas or air can be pumped inside the airship from one airtight-fabric cell to another. This makes the airship tilt nose-up or tail-up, for climbing and descending.

SPORTS BALLOONS
Balloons are used for fun, sport and for record-breaking attempts. They are filled with gases such as helium, or hot air from a burner. Hot air rises because it is lighter and less dense than normal air.

BASKET AND BURNER
The hot-air balloon's lightweight basket is made of woven wickerwork with strengthening wooden strips and strakes. Hot air comes from the flame of a propane-gas burner, fueled from high-pressure bottles.

Flame outlet

Fuel line

Burner

Padded rim

Glossary

Airfoil The specially curved shape of an airplane wing. It produces an upward force or lift as it moves through the air.

Aft Towards the rear.

Aileron One of the airplane's main control surfaces, usually mounted at the back of the outer part of the main wing. It makes the plane tilt, roll and turn.

Biplane An airplane with two main pairs of wings, one above the other.

Bulkhead A major structural part, usually inside a fuselage. It separates the fuselage into sections and gives it shape and strength. *See also former.*

Center section The central part joining the two wings. In many airplanes it is part of the fuselage.

Chord The 'width' of a wing, from front to back.

Control surface A flat part that tilts into the air flowing past an airplane, and controls the plane's position and direction. *See aileron, elevator and rudder.*

Delta wings Triangle-shaped wings, as on the Concorde.

Drag The force encountered as an airplane pushes through the air, which tends to slow it down.

Elevator One of the airplane's main control surfaces, usually mounted on the fin. It makes the plane climb or descend.

Fin The flat part usually near the rear end of an airplane, sometimes called the vertical stabilizer or 'tail'. It usually carries the rudder.

Former Part of a structure that gives shape to the whole structure. Inside a fuselage, for example, formers provide the tubular shape. They are not as strong as bulkheads, but they are stronger than hoops.

Forward Towards the front.

Fuselage The central 'body' of the plane, to which the wings and fins are attached. It is usually shaped like a tapering tube, with the pilot and controls near the front.

Hoops (rings) Ring-shaped parts that help to give the fuselage its tube shape. *See also former.*

Hydraulic Working by high-pressure fluid.

Jack A hydraulic piston and cylinder, that pushes on a part such as a landing wheel or control surface, and moves it.

Leading edge The front edge or part, especially of a wing, tailplane or fin.

Lift An upward force that causes an object to rise. In aircraft it may be produced by downward-facing propellers, or by a moving wing with an airfoil shape.

Light plane A type of general-purpose small plane with one or two propeller-driving engines, and seats for a few passsengers.

Longeron A strong strip or girder that runs front-to-back inside the fuselage, to give it strength along its length. *See also stringer.*

Monoplane An airplane with one pair of main wings, like most modern planes.

Pitch The lengthways angle of an airplane compared to the horizontal, that is, whether the plane is flying level, climbing or diving. In helicopters, the angle of the rotor blade is called the pitch.

Propeller A screw-shaped device that turns rapidly and forces air past it, like a fan. A propeller on an airplane propels it along by pulling or pushing the surrounding air. Sometimes called an airscrew.

Rib A curved part inside a wing, that gives the wing its strength and airfoil shape from front to back.

Roll The side-to-side angle of an airplane compared to the horizontal.

Rudder One of the airplane's main control surfaces, usually mounted on the fin. It makes the plane turn left or right.

Shaft A central bar on which, for example, a turbine is fixed.

Spar A long strip or girder inside a part such as a wing or fin, that gives it stiffness and strength all along its length.

Spigot A knob-like projection on one part that fits into a hole in another part, to fit the two parts together accurately.

Spoiler A panel usually near the trailing edge of a wing, that spoils the airflow over it. It is part of the control surface system.

Stringer A bar or strip that runs lengthways inside a part such as a fuselage or wing. It maintains the part's shape and adds some strength, but not as much strength as a longeron.

Strut Any strip, bar or girder that adds strength and shape to a part, or holds one part away from another.

Tailplane The smaller horizontal wing, generally near the back of an airplane. It usually carries the elevators.

Trailing edge The rear edge or part, especially of a wing, tailplane or fin.

Trim The fine details of an airplane's balance and flight, so that when all the controls are set at their middle or neutral positions the plane flies straight and level.

Turbine A set of fan-shaped blades on a shaft that spin in moving air (or water), or spin to move air (or water) past them.

Turbofan A type of jet engine with a huge turbine fan at the front, used on most modern large jet planes.

Yaw The direction an airplane points in, that is, whether it is turning left or right.

Index